Helion & Company Limited
Unit 8 Amherst Business Centre
Budbrooke Road
Warwick
CV34 5WE
England
Tel. 01926 499 619
Email: info@helion.co.uk
Website: www.helion.co.uk
Twitter: @helionbooks
Visit our blog http://blog.helion.co.uk/

Text © Krzysztof Dabrowski 2020
Photographs © as individually credited
Colour profiles © David Bocquelet and Tom
Cooper 2020
Maps © Tom Cooper 2020

Designed & typeset by Farr out Publications,
    Wokingham, Berkshire
Cover design Paul Hewitt, Battlefield Design
    (www.battlefield-design.co.uk)
Printed by Henry Ling Limited, Dorchester,
    Dorset

ISBN 978-1-913118-68-6

British Library Cataloguing-in-Publication
    Data
A catalogue record for this book is available
    from the British Library

We always welcome receiving book
proposals from prospective authors.

CONTENTS

For ease of understanding, the official names of the two Chinese states – the People's
Republic of China (PRC) on the Asian continent (also 'mainland China'), and the Republic of
China (ROC) on the island of Taiwan – are given as in official use. Although the term 'China'
and 'Chinese' applies for both places, terms such as 'Taiwan' and 'Taiwanese' are used for
reasons of clarity within the given context.

ABBREVIATIONS

AA	anti-aircraft
AAA	anti-aircraft artillery
AAM	air-to-air missile
AB	air base
AD	air defence
AFB	Air Force Base
ASCC	Air Standardisation Coordinating Committee
CIA	Central Intelligence Agency
C-in-C	commander in chief
c/n	construction number
CO	commanding officer
COMINT	communications intelligence
ECM	electronic countermeasures
ECCM	electronic counter-countermeasures
ELINT	electronic intelligence
EW	electronic warfare
FSB	Federalnaya Sluzhba Bezopasnosti – Federal Security Service (the main internal security agency of the Russian Federation since 1991)
GenShtab	Soviet General Staff (equivalent to the Joint Chiefs of Staff in the USA)
GIAP	Gvardeyskiy Istrebitelniy Aviatsionniy Polk – Guards Fighter Aviation Regiment (Soviet tactical fighter unit)
GCI	Ground Control Intercept
HUMINT	human intelligence
HQ	headquarters
IAF	Indian Air Force
IAP	Istrebitelniy Aviatsionniy Polk – Fighter Aviation Regiment (Soviet tactical fighter unit)
IFF	Identification Friend or Foe
JCS	Joint Chiefs of Staff (US armed forces)
KGB	Komitet Gosudarstvennoy Bezopasnosti – State Security Comitee (the main external and internal

	security agency of the Soviet Union until 1991)
MiG	Mikoyan i Gurevich (the design bureau led by Artyom Ivanovich Mikoyan and Mikhail Iosifovich Gurevich, also known as OKB-155 or MMZ 'Zenit')
NATO	North Atlantic Treaty Organization
NSA	National Security Agency (USA)
PHOTOINT	photographic intelligence
PLA	People's Liberation Army
PLAAF	People's Liberation Army Air Force
PVO	see V-PVO
PRC	People's Republic of China
R-3S	Soviet short-range AAM (ASCC codename AA-2 Atoll)
RAF	Royal Air Force (of the United Kingdom)
ROC	Republic of China
ROCAF	Republic of China Air Force
SAC	Strategic Air Command
SAGW	surface-to-air guided weapon
SAM	surface-to-air missile
SIGINT	signals intelligence
SRW	Strategic Reconnaissance Wing
Su	Sukhoi (the design bureau led by Pavel Ossipovich Sukhoi, also known as OKB-51)
TFW	Tactical Fighter Wing
UAV	Unmanned Aerial Vehicle
UFO	unidentified flying object
US/USA	United States of America
USAF	United States Air Force
USN	United States Navy
USSR	Union of Soviet Socialist Republics
V-PVO	Voyska Protivovozdushnoy Oborny (Soviet Air Defence Forces or Anti-Air Defence Troops; also PVO strany).
WRS/P	Weather Reconnaissance Squadron/Provisional

PREFACE AND ACKNOWLEDGEMENTS

The Lockheed U-2 high altitude renaissance aircraft and Soviet-made surface-to-air missiles (SAMs) – or, more precisely, the bold but provocative missions flown by the former, and the attempts to counter them by the letter – have epitomized the rivalry between the United States of America (USA), and the Union of Soviet Socialist Republics (USSR/Soviet Union) during the early to middle Cold War period, both within the realms of the aviation and as a whole. The purpose of this volume is not to provide an exhaustive developmental history of either, as this has been done often before: instead, and while detailing their coming-into-being, the primary aim of this study is to provide a succinct, yet detailed account of how their confrontations played out and, last but not least, what kind of impact they had upon the not so distant history of warfare and military aviation in particular.

Before getting to the point an important issue deserves to be addressed when dealing with intelligence-gathering missions flown by US aircraft and U-2 overflights. The term 'reconnaissance aircraft' and 'reconnaissance mission' is used consistently instead of 'spy aircraft' or 'spying'. Collecting intelligence by means of aircraft was frequently termed 'spying', whereas what actually took place in the cases described below was far away from any kind of 'shady' activity, no matter how secretive. The men who performed the missions in question were pilots employed by intelligence services or military forces to fly aircraft taking photographs or employing other means of intelligence gathering, and by no means dishonourable characters hatching nefarious plots to extract information. The aircraft they flew were military aircraft designed to fly at very high altitudes, almost outside the limits of airspace, and often using military means of electronic deception – these were not passenger or sports aircraft gathering intelligence under the cover of civilian status. Therefore, the use of terms like 'spy', 'spying', 'spy aircraft' and similar, would not do justice to the men and their equipment; indeed, it would be entirely out of place.

As usual, a research project of this kind is very much the result of lots of teamwork. In this case, it would not have been possible without consistent encouragement, advice, and practical help from Dymitry Zubkov, Chris Pocock, Tom Cooper, Albert Grandolini, Antoine Pierre, and Yufei Mao, to all of whom I would like to express my most sincere gratitude.

INTRODUCTION

Once the Second World War was concluded, erstwhile allies in the East and the West swiftly became rivals and enemies due to insurmountable differences of political nature, as well as directly opposed ambitions. The guns had hardly fallen silent in Europe when US reconnaissance aircraft and Soviet fighters clashed. These early encounters were more or less accidental and comparable to cases of amicide between Soviet and US aircraft during the war itself. However because of the aforementioned post-war enmity between the Soviet Union and the United States (and by extension their respective allies and satellite states), in particular a perceived military threat from the East, the United States sought to gather data concerning the Soviet military including the size, composition and the disposition of its forces and to gather information regarding military facilities (for example air bases), dual use infrastructure such as road and rail networks, industrial installations as well as anything else that might be of intelligence value. The importance of obtaining data to avoid a surprise attack from the east was obvious but it should be noted that as well as being of a defensive nature, and arguably dictated by a sense of self-preservation, it also had the potential to serve offensive purposes (though, of course, the United States did not initiate a war of aggression against the Soviet Union even when it enjoyed a nuclear monopoly). While the necessity of gathering intelligence hardly needs further justification from a Western point of view it has to be added that because of the secretive and closed nature of the Soviet Union (and the Eastern Bloc by extension) the said data had to be obtained by using reconnaissance aircraft which were in most cases the only means to effectively do so.[1]

Concerning the aforementioned intelligence gathering aerial activity, by late 1946 the US Army Air Force (which was not yet a wholly independent arm of service) began conducting reconnaissance missions along the borders of the Soviet Union and its satellite states. In the course of these flights electronic and photographic intelligence could be collected, but due to the manner in which the missions were flown their coverage was limited to only the peripheral regions of the potential enemy. Meanwhile, in 1947 the United States Air Force (USAF) was formed as a separate service. Its commanders soon began seeking authorisation to not only reconnoitre peripheral areas but to conduct direct overflights of Soviet territory itself. However, the Joint Chiefs of Staff (JCS) after consulting with, among others, the secretaries of defence and state, denied these requests. Moreover, after in 1948 the Soviet foreign ministry protested alleged intrusions of what were termed "bombers" over Soviet territorial waters, the Department of State in Washington insisted on restricting reconnaissance missions in such a manner as not to approach Soviet borders and territorial waters any closer than 40 miles. Direct overflights would thus be out of the question. Nevertheless, the US armed forces and intelligence services continued issuing requests for permission for overflights of Soviet territory. Responding to one of these in October 1950 the USAF director of intelligence, Major-General Charles P Cabell replied that he would have to recommend against it, adding at the same time that a day may come when the overflights become either more essential or less objectionable. This day came before long.

Partially in response to the situation developing after the outbreak of the Korean War, in December 1950 US President Henry Truman authorised direct overflights of the Soviet Union. While the outbreak of war in the Far East without doubt accelerated the decision-making process, the Americans and the West in general grew increasingly apprehensive concerning the Soviet Union's development of nuclear weapons (the first Soviet atomic bomb was detonated in 1949), radars, missiles, and strategic bombers, as well as other advanced weapons and systems. Therefore, it was only a matter of time before – in the absence of other means of collecting intelligence – direct overflights of the Soviet territory became an indispensable necessity.

Of course, the Soviets were keen to undertake everything in their powers to shoot down any intruders in their airspace, which in turn meant that aerial missions taking US and – in lesser numbers – British aircraft over the USSR were hazardous. The Western allies thus sought for ways to make their aircraft as hard to detect, track and intercept as possible. One of the earliest solutions were nocturnal operations at low altitude. As the Soviet radar network began to improve, US and British reconnaissance aircraft began flying at ever higher altitudes, because as of the early 1950s, detection and interception of high-flying aircraft confronted the Soviets with numerous challenges. Moreover, aerostats were used extensively: for example in 1947 the US Navy launched Project Skyhawk, in the course of which it made extensive use of plastic (polyethylene) balloons carrying reconnaissance cameras and released to altitudes of up to 30,000 metres (98,000ft) – above the reach of Soviet air defences. The US Air Force followed in fashion in 1950 when it used strong western winds to release reconnaissance balloons – so-called 'spy blimps' – from several points in Western Europe into the skies over the Soviet-controlled Eastern Europe and the USSR.

While, on a humorous side, some of the aerostats resulted in reported sightings of the so-called unidentified flying objects (UFOs), they were not taken lightly by the Soviets and their East European allies: dozens of fighters were scrambled to intercept them, and dozens of spy blimps were shot down. Yet, because they could not be steered, many more disappeared without trace, while those eventually recovered 'on the other side' of the USSR, often delivered disappointing results. Even so, they were not taken lightly by the Soviets: just like overflights by manned aircraft, they frequently drew angry condemnations from Moscow.

On 4 February 1956, Moscow issued one demarche against overflights by US-made aerostats; another, especially strong protest was delivered by Soviet representatives to the USA on 14 December 1956, following an overflight of Soviet territory by three US aircraft three days earlier. As the Soviets became ever more vocal, they eventually prompted US President Dwight D Eisenhower to order his Secretary of Defense, Charles Wilson, the JCS Chairman General Nathan Twining, and the director of the Central Intelligence Agency (CIA) Allen Dulles, to immediately cease further violations of the airspace over the USSR and allied countries in Eastern Europe.

Predating this order, during the Four Powers Summit held in Geneva, in Switzerland, in July 1955, Eisenhower made a public offer to the Soviets, known as the 'Open Skies': his idea was for both the West and the East to permit reconnaissance overflights as a mutual confidence-building measure. However, the deeply mistrusting

Soviets turned this offer down. Their mistrust was not without a reason: although the US president subsequently ordered US services to cease reconnaissance missions over the USSR and its allies, this rule remained valid for only a short while. Before long a novel and secret aircraft with unmatched capabilities for high-altitude operations entered testing – which revealed that it was about to provide the US services with the ability to conduct photographic reconnaissance missions over the Soviet Union without the fear of being opposed, at least not for the time being.

1

RIVALS

Thus far, except for the Soviet protests mentioned above, only the American side of the story has been narrated. However, as in any conflict, it is important to the consider point of view of all the parties involved – in this case the Soviets. This is where it is necessary to look back at the Second World War – or the Great Patriotic War, as this conflict was known in the USSR – fought from 1941 until 1945. Not only was the Soviet Union was taken by surprise and then suffered catastrophic losses when invaded by Nazi Germany on 22 June 1941: throughout most of this war, high-flying reconnaissance aircraft of the Luftwaffe proved capable of flying deep into Soviet airspace and returning unmolested. Not only were such aircraft out of reach of contemporary anti-aircraft artillery, but they were a difficult target even for fast interceptors. The situation reached the point where a successful interception of such aircraft – not to mention their successful downing – was considered a particularly noteworthy achievement. Unsurprisingly, the Soviets realised very early on that reconnaissance aircraft underway at high-altitude presented a particular challenge for any kind of air defences. Of course, the introduction to service of jet-powered aircraft after 1945 only exasperated the problem. Moreover, it was not only reconnaissance aircraft that constituted a problem: high-flying bombers were at least as much of a threat, and this was further multiplied considering at the time these tended to fly in large formations. Strength lay in numbers when one was bombing conventionally: the devastation that could be caused by heavy bombers was multiplied by the number of aircraft in every formation. Worse yet, by 1945, a single bomber became capable of eradicating an entire city by the means of just one nuclear bomb – in turn making it clear that in any future war the Soviets and their allies would have to make sure they could not only intercept, but also shoot down every single intruder of their airspace.

S-25: The first Soviet Surface-to-Air Missile System

Facing the threat of thousands of US and allied bombers and reconnaissance aircraft, the Soviets launched feverish work on improving their air defences during the late 1940s. The first obvious option was to design and manufacture jet powered fighter-interceptors

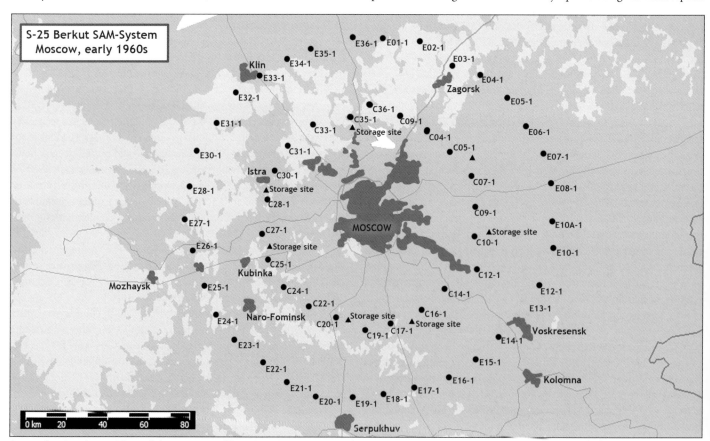

A map showing the positions of the two rings of S-25/SA-1 SAM-sites around Moscow containing a total of 56 sites. Each site included one B-200 fire control radar and 60 V-300 launchers and missiles. The deployment of the S-25 eventually led to the construction of two main rings of highways around the Soviet/Russian capital. (Map by Tom Cooper, based on Fowler)

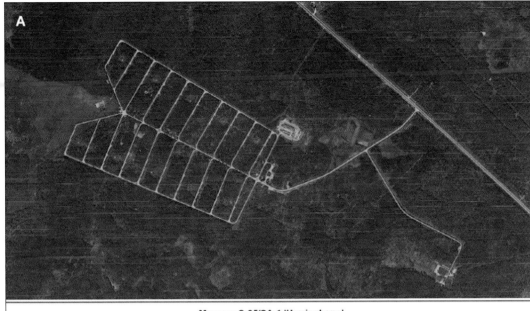

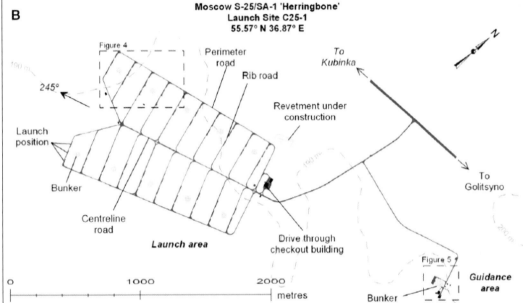

A KH-7 GAMBIT satellite photograph and a corresponding interpretation of an S-25/SA-1 SAM-site, C25-1, outside Moscow. (Courtesy Fowler)

efforts produced an operational system before the German capitulation on 8 May 1945 (or 9 May, from the Soviet point of view), the scientists involved had undertaken much research, development, and testing. When the Soviets overran the eastern part of Germany, they thus acquired much of the resulting know-how, and this formed a solid base to start from.

Certainly enough, the history of early Soviet surface-to-air missile development included ample political machinations, favouritism and nepotism. As such, it is much too long to be related in a succinct manner here. In this place, it is sufficient to say that the traditional body bridging the national security strategy and the military operational art is the General Staff of the Armed Forces (Generalnny Stab, or GenShtab). Established (or re-organised) in 1935, the GenShtab is a body staffed by a 'caste' of professional planners: hand-picked military brains never rotated through any other assignments and thus never becoming 'attached' to a specific branch of the armed forces. While having no operational control of the force, it is responsible for *all* planning at operational and strategic levels, working as doctrine and capability developer, and as the sole procurement authority.

In other words: the GenShtab is what was frequently – and often cryptically – reported as being the 'Soviet military theoreticians' over the last 70 years.

On a direct order from Joseph Vissarionovich Stalin (general secretary of the Communist Party of the Soviet Union and premier of the Soviet Union – and thus the Soviet leader – from the mid-1920s until his death in 1953), issued in August 1950, the GenShtab formed the Special (Design) Bureau No.1 (SB-1), with the task of developing an operational SAM system. The first to reach technical maturity was the S-25 Berkut. Developed with the aim of facilitating the air defence of Moscow, its workability was proven in a series of tests culminating on 26 April 1953 when a remotely-controlled Tupolev Tu-4 target drone (actually a Soviet "clone" of the American Boeing B-29 bomber) was shot down over the Kapustin Yar missile test range.[2]

More tests followed under varying conditions including the simultaneous engagement of multiple targets demonstrating that the system was sufficiently developed for operational deployment. Although already technically obsolete, the system was rushed into production and then into service. The first units were deployed in March 1954 and went on alert in June 1956: eventually, the Soviets

with much improved performance: aircraft capable of reaching ever higher speeds and ever higher altitudes. Moreover, such aircraft then had to be equipped with systems enabling them to be efficiently guided into the interception, with on-board sensors enabling them to find their targets and – to ease the actual act of interception – then be equipped with guided air-to-air missiles capable of knocking out the enemy aircraft with a single blow. Correspondingly, the development of new and improved fighter-interceptors was only a part of the solution: their operations required a much-improved system of ground-based radars and communication facilities.[1]

Apart from fielding high performance fighter-interceptors, another approach to dealing with the problem of high-flying bombers and reconnaissance aircraft was to develop guided surface-to-air missiles (SAMs). While such a project was particularly challenging from a technical point of view, the Soviets had the benefit of capturing extensive documentation about missile technology from the former Nazi Germany: during the last three years of the Second World War, the latter found itself confronted with ever more massive Allied bombing raids, and thus invested heavily in the development of several types of guided surface-to-air missiles. While none of the related

A V-300 missile with its launcher pad (which also served as a transport trolley) in the launch position. (Illustrated Guide to Moscow Anti-Aircraft Defense System)

The launch of a V-300 missile. (Illustrated Guide to Moscow Anti-Aircraft Defense System)

constructed two fixed defensive rings containing a total of 56 batteries (or sites) around Moscow. Each of these included its own B-200 radar bunker, 60 launch pads and all the necessary support equipment. Due to built-in redundancy and overlapping engagement zones each of the S-25 SAM-sites could simultaneously engage up to 20 targets.

From S-25 to S/SA-75

As much as the successful fielding of the S-25 surface-to-air missile system was a noteworthy achievement, its limitations and disadvantages became apparent even before it was fully deployed. For one, the system utilised a single stage missile, which negatively impacted its performance: the V-300 was slow in acceleration, had an effective engagement range of only about 25 kilometres, and there were doubts about its effectiveness against supersonic targets. Foremost: S-25 Berkut was consuming gargantuan amounts of resources to be put into place – just to provide anti-aircraft defences for a single location (even if that was considered to be the most important one). Being immobile it could not be redeployed anywhere else, while the enormous costs required to set it up excluded the possibility of fielding a second system of this type to defend even a single other city or major installation. In a country as huge as the USSR, with numerous major population centres, strategically-important facilities and military bases, there was a dire need for protection from aerial reconnaissance and potential attack. An alternative, simpler solution to the problem of providing ground-based air defences was thus urgently required.

While work on the S-25 Berkut was still in progress the Kremlin ordered the development of new, less-expensive systems. However, the development of a cheaper, rail-mobile version designated the S-50, for the protection of Leningrad, was abandoned. The same happened to a more sophisticated system developed by the famous fighter-designer Lavochkin, codenamed Dal: this was cancelled in the early 1960s. Instead, a secondary yet more economical and much more flexible air defence system was designed by a team under Boris Bunkin at the KB-1 Almaz bureau, starting in 1953. Parallel research on a new low-frequency fire-control radar, and the emergence of a new, two-stage ShB-32 missile designed by Lavochkin's former deputies now regrouped within the OKB-2 design bureau (which subsequently became known under the designation Fakel), resulted in the emergence of an entirely new SAM-system, designated 'S-75 Volga'.

Technically, the S-75 was a major leap forward in comparison to the S-25: while still having the strategic defence of major urban areas and military facilities against high-flying aircraft as its primary purpose, it used a lot of new technology and was much more flexible. Contrary to the S-25, which was deployed in huge and fixed sites, all the major components of the S-75 were installed on trucks or tractors and semi-trailers, making it transportable – even if at a relatively slow rate: all the equipment of just one main tactical combat unit (a battalion or 'SAM-site') weighed well over 100 tonnes. Its main component was the RSN-75 fire-control, tracking and guidance unit. Supported by three other radars, and controlled from the command post, this served the purpose of engaging one target at time with up to six (though usually only two or three) liquid-fuelled 1D missiles. The latter were big, two-staged weapons, launched from one of six SM-63 single-rail launchers assigned to every battery. These were usually deployed following a hexagonal pattern, consisting of earth- or sand berms, intersected by roads used for moving reload missiles and support equipment: this became one of the S-75's easiest-to-recognise characteristics.[3]

Highly promising, the S-75 was rushed into mass production even before officially accepted for service, on 11 December 1957: the original plan was to manufacture no fewer than 265 SAM-sites and 7,220 V-750 missiles between 1956 and 1960. The baseline SA-75 Dvina version, with the V-750V/11D missile, entered service in 1957, followed by the S-75N Desna, with V-750VN/13D missile, a

Terminology and Designations

For the better understanding of terminology and designations used by the Soviets, and by its opponents in the West, it is necessary to understand that in the armed forces of the former Soviet Union, most heavy SAM-systems like the S-25 Berkut were operated by the Soviet Air Defence Forces or Anti-Air Defence Troops (Voyska Protivovozdushnoy Oborny, V-PVO, or PVO strany). The principal combat unit operating S-25s in the V-PVO was a *divizion* – a word that in the Soviet/Russian, and some other Eastern, militaries denotes what is called an artillery battalion in the West (regardless of whether equipped with tube-artillery, rockets, or missiles). Obviously, *divizion* is sometimes wrongly translated from Russian into English as 'division', although – bar phonetic semblance, of course – it has nothing in common with the large (multi-brigade or multi-regiment) military unit: actually, it is a battalion-sized unit. As with other militaries, the V-PVO's battalions were regularly organised into units of higher order, such as regiments, brigades, divisions and corps. To avoid any possible confusion, in this book, V-PVO's *divizions* are denoted either as missile battalions, SAM-batteries or SAM-sites.

Another terminology-related issue is that of the original weapon system designations of the Soviets and their nomenclature in the West. The Soviets used to have at least three distinct weapon designation systems of their own, each of which followed entirely different formats. While many details about these remain controversial, it is certain that one was based on the designer's designation and usually started with the word '*Izdeliye*'; the second was used by the military to designate entire weapons systems (for example: not only the specific missile, bomb or otherwise, but also including the platform deploying it), and the third was used to designate specific elements – or modifications – of various weapon systems.

The majority of Soviet designations remained unknown in the West well into the 1990s, i.e. until after the end of the Cold War. The US and allied intelligence services experienced the very same problem with identification of Soviet weapons system as they had experienced with Japanese weapon systems during the Second World War. Correspondingly, a practice invented in 1942 was adopted according to which enemy aircraft – and then subsequently other weapons systems – were systematically assigned code-names. Early during the Cold War the related decisions were the task of the Air Standards Co-ordinating Committee (ASCC), formed by the USA, United Kingdom, Canada, Australia and New Zealand. The ASCC's system of simple, easy to memorise codenames for aircraft depending on their purpose was then adopted throughout the armed forces of the countries that joined the North Atlantic Treaty Organisation (NATO) in the mid-1950s, where it was further developed to also include systematic codenames for rockets and missiles.

Thus the S-25 Berkut was designated 'SA-1 Guild' by the ASCC, and then NATO. Similarly, its follow-up, the S/SA-75 family of SAM-systems and associated equipment were codenamed 'SA-2 Guideline'. While the 'SA' used by the ASCC/NATO came from 'surface-to-air', and codenames starting with 'g' stood for 'guided missile', Western codenames for radars supporting the S-25 and S/SA-75 were less systematic: for example, the B-200 fire-control radar and guidance system of the S-25 was codenamed 'Yo-Yo' by US intelligence, while the SNR-75 fire-control radar of the S/SA-75 SAM-system became known as the 'Fan Song'.

An A-100 Kama radar station of the S-25 Berkut/SA-1 Guild SAM-system. (Illustrated Guide to Moscow Anti-Aircraft Defense System)

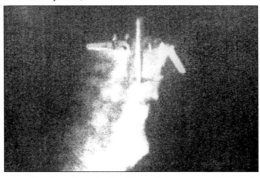

A still from a film showing the downing of a Tu-4 target drone by a V-300 missile. (Illustrated Guide to Moscow Anti-Aircraft Defense System)

year later – although both took nearly a year to get officially accepted for operational use. By 1961, a total of no less than 435 batteries was in service.[4]

While production was still ramping up, further research and development resulted in the emergence of additional variants. Already in 1958, the development of the first major modification, the S-75M Volkhov system including the much-improved RSN-75V radar (capable of simultaneously tracking up to six targets) and SM-90 launchers, was authorised. Similarly, multiple improved variants of the original 1D missile – which had a maximum engagement range of 29,000m (18 miles) and maximum engagement altitude of 23,000m (95,144ft) – emerged by 1960, the two of which, V-750V/11D and the V-75VN/13D, proved capable of reaching as high as 29,000m (95,144ft). That said, the basic essence of every S-75 system, regardless of the variant, always remained the same: the centrepiece of each was the RSN-75 or RSNA-75 fire-control radar. Supported by an early warning radar and a height-finding radar, and controlled from the command post, this served the purpose of engaging one target at a time with up to six (though usually three) missiles fired from one of six single-rail launchers.

Table 1: Major Early Versions of the S-75 SAM-System

	Fire-Control Radar	Primary Missile	Notes
SA-75 Dvina	RSNA-75	V-750/1D and V-750V/11D	Low-frequency radar; in service 1957
S-75N Desna	RSN-75	V-750VN/13D	High-frequency radar; in service 1958
S-75M Volkhov	RSN-75V	V-755/20D and V-760/15D	High-frequency radar; in service 1960

Table 2: Early Missiles of the S-75 System

Missile	Factory Index	Notes
V-750	1D	Range 29,000m; maximum altitude 23,000m
V-750V	11D	Range 29,000m, maximum altitude 25,000m
V-750VM	11DM	Home-on-jam variant
V-750VN	13D	Range 29,000m, maximum altitude 25,000m
V-760	15D	Nuclear warhead
V-755	20D	Range 43,000m, maximum altitude 30,000m

Table 3: Equipment of a typical S-75 SAM-site of the V-PVO, 1958-1962

Equipment and Remarks	Number of Systems per SAM-Site/ Battalion
UV fire-control station (command post)	1
P-10 (ASCC/NATO-codename 'Knife Rest') VHF-band early warning radar (range 75km/47nm)	1
P-12 (ASCC/NATO-codename 'Spoon Rest') C-band acquisition radar (range 200km)	1
PRV-10 (ASCC/NATO-codename 'Rock Cake') or PRV-11 ('Side Net') E-band height-finding radar (range 200km/124nm or 240km/149nm respectively)	1
RSN-75 or RSNA-75 (ASCC/NATO-codename 'Fan Song') E/F/G-band fire-control radar (detection range 140km/87nm; acquisition range 100km/62nm); capable of simultaneously tracking up to six targets, but engaging only one at a time	1
SM-63-I launcher	6
PR-11 transporter-loaders (each with one spare missile)	3

U-2: a legend is born

Voluminous works have been written providing intricate detail on the research and development of the Lockheed U-2 high-altitude reconnaissance aircraft. Trying to match them in a few paragraphs would be rather pointless: nevertheless, the type does require at least a brief introduction.[5]

Arguably one of the world's most famous reconnaissance aircraft had its origin in the US Air Force's Design Study Requirements of 27 March 1953. The said document called for an aircraft with an operational radius of 1,500 nautical miles (about 2,778 kilometres) 70,000 feet (over 21,000 meters) – or higher – operational ceiling, a subsonic speed, one-man crew and a payload of reconnaissance equipment of between 100 and up to 700 pounds (45-318Kg). The basic idea was to obtain an aircraft with such characteristics that this could operate above the reach of Soviet air defences and, it was expected, even outside the upper limits of their radar-detection and tracking capabilities. Several aviation companies were approached in this regard and in due time submitted their proposals: left out was the Lockheed Aircraft Corporation, which – nevertheless – learned of the Air Force's requirement and on 18 May 1954 presented an unsolicited design which was the work of the corporation's best aircraft designer, Clarence L. Kelly Johnson.

Originally known as the CL-282, the Lockheed design was, essentially, a jet-powered sailplane with long, slender wings and a relatively short fuselage. Of note is that the power plant originally chosen by the designer was the J-73 turbojet, and that the aircraft was not intended to have a traditional landing gear. This unorthodox concept was presented to the US Air Force (USAF) but was negatively received. Indeed, on 7 June 1954, Johnson was informed by letter that his proposal had been rejected. However, not all was lost, for while the military establishment was not interested in his design a certain civilian agency would be very much so.

To make a long story short, the matter concerning a novel and unconventional reconnaissance aircraft reached the highest possible

'The Article': the first U-2 prototype as seen during testing at 'Area 51'. (National Museum of the US Air Force)

level – the President of the United States. While the exact date could not be determined – it is only certain that this decision was taken in November 1954 – President Eisenhower personally approved the development of the aircraft, stipulating that it should be handled in an unconventional way, so as to avoid it becoming entangled in bureaucracy or stalled by rivalries among the services. The president's will resulted in the signing of a US$54 million contract for the production of 20 aircraft, on 9 December 1954. While their general layout was to remain as described in the previous paragraph, the J-57 engine was adopted instead, and a wheeled undercarriage added.

On 24 July 1955 the first Lockheed high altitude reconnaissance aircraft – meanwhile officially designated U-2A – arrived at the Groom Lake test site inside a restricted area ('Area 51'), approximately 100 miles (some 160 kilometres) northwest of Las Vegas, Nevada. Like all the early examples, it was powered by Pratt & Whitney J-57-P37 engines, which proved fuel efficient but also difficult to re-light if flamed out at high altitude. Static engine run-ups were conducted on 27 July 1955 and the aircraft taxied on the ground for the first time on 29 July, with Lockheed test pilot Tony LeVier in the cockpit. During subsequent taxiing tests the aircraft unintentionally lifted off the ground, though this did not result in serious damage: instead, it provided valuable lessons concerning its handling and resulted in the

introduction of several modifications. The first proper flight of the U-2 took place on 4 August 1955 with LeVier at the controls. Four days later, on 8 August, the aircraft was flown again by the same pilot, and made the first official presentation flight to senior CIA officials.

More testing followed, and many of the modifications found necessary were applied. Naturally, numerous difficulties were encountered and accidents happened – including fatal crashes. Nevertheless, the USA eventually found itself in possession of a reconnaissance aircraft capable of operating at 72,000 feet (about 22,000 meters) and fitted with high resolution cameras allowing it to conduct quality photographic reconnaissance. Apart from these obvious advantages the U-2 had certain weaknesses, too. The most obvious was that of its configuration as – essentially – a jet-powered glider: this required the pilot to handle it differently than most aircraft, a skill that in turn required thorough training. Another potentially problematic issue was the fact that the aircraft had a fragile, light-weight structure, required to lessen the weight, and that there was little that Lockheed could do to fully alleviate that. Nevertheless, by late 1955 and early 1956 it became obvious that the U-2 program was reaching sufficient maturity to facilitate the aircraft's operational deployment. This was to follow shortly.

2
EARLY U-2 OVERFLIGHTS

Before the initial experiences with the CIA-operated U-2s are described in detail, one needs to keep in mind the issue of pilots selected to fly the type for the top US intelligence agency. While certainly a welcome feature, the U-2's – theoretic – immunity to interception by Soviet air defences was no guarantee of absolute safety: indeed, its operations could not but be described as inherently dangerous, because most of these were to be undertaken directly over 'enemy' territory. Unsurprisingly, at least early on, the CIA played with the idea of hiring foreign pilots to fly the type. For a number of reasons, this idea came to nought: although a few British and Taiwanese pilots were to be trained on the U-2 later on, it would be the Americans that were to fly the type into Soviet airspace. The next issue was that of their selection: because President Eisenhower expressed his 'firm

wish' that their overflights to be run as a 'civilian operation', and because a US military operation inside Soviet airspace would legally represent an act of war, they could not be active military pilots, nor wear the uniforms of the US armed forces. Furthermore, even pilots that would resign their commission from the armed services were out of the question – foremost because such resignations necessitated a bureaucratically complicated procedure. The CIA's solution was to recruit reservist pilots of the USAF: in that way, they were – at least officially – 'civilians', while in turn the USAF pledged that it would later permit the involved pilots to re-join their service at the same rank.

Distribution of Responsibilities

Although the Americans flying the U-2s over the USSR were thus – at least officially – to be civilians, their operations still required the cooperation and support of the USAF. The latter was to select and train all the pilots for the CIA's U-2-programme, and to plan their missions, while the Central Intelligence Agency was responsible for handling cameras and processing films, arranging bases abroad, and – last but not least – to ensure project security. Even then, it promptly became obvious that, regardless of how tight the security was, the project could not be kept entirely secret. For this reason, the CIA launched a cover-story, the so-called 'legend', according to which the Lockheed-developed aircraft was to be flown by the USAF Air Weather Service on behalf of the National Advisory Committee on Aeronautics (NACS), for the purpose of studying jet-streams, convective clouds, temperatures, cosmic-ray effects, and wind changes at high altitudes. Indeed, the U-2 prototypes even carried NACA instruments during their initial flights and collected precious information that was quickly handed over to that body for further evaluation.

Finally, there was the issue of what to do should one of the U-2s go down while underway over unfriendly territory. One of the first ideas was for the US officials to be straightforward and state that it was a reconnaissance aircraft. Eventually, the solution of declaring the aircraft as involved in 'high altitude weather reconnaissance' prevailed instead.

Initially, the CIA planned to run its U-2 operations from Great Britain, and picked Royal Air Force (RAF) Lakenheath as its main base for what was officially announced as the 1st Weather Reconnaissance Squadron, Provisional (WRS/P-1). The unit began deploying to Lakenheath on 29 April 1956, and by 4 May of the same year was fully deployed there, including four U-2 aircraft and all the necessary support personnel. When the first flight from this base was undertaken still remains unclear, but it is known that one of the early training missions prompted the RAF to scramble four of its own interceptors on 18 May 1956. What is also known is that no operational sorties were conducted from Lakenheath at this stage: all flights served the purpose of testing the reassembled aircraft or the training of pilots. For a number of reasons, it was decided to re-deploy the U-2s to Wiesbaden in what was then West Germany – a location that had both advantages and disadvantages: while Wiesbaden was one of the busiest airfields in that part of Europe, and thus avoiding undue attention was certainly expected to become difficult, it was close to Camp King, a major US intelligence facility. This is how Wiesbaden, and not Lakenheath became the staging base for a number of early U-2 operations.

Initial U-2 Operations

All the efforts by the CIA, Lockheed, and the involved personnel finally began to bear fruit on 20 June 1956, when the first operational high-altitude photographic reconnaissance sortie – Mission 2003 – was flown by a U-2. Equipped only with A2 high-resolution cameras, and piloted by Carl K Overstreet, the aircraft flew from Wiesbaden over Czechoslovakia and Poland (including their respective capitals, Prague and Warsaw), before skimming East Germany on the way back – all without incident. More importantly, the photographic material obtained in the course of Mission 2003 was gauged as of 'high quality'. Two additional sorties are known to have been flown over Eastern Bloc countries shortly after: on 2 July 1956, Missions 2009 and 2010 covered most of Rumania, Bulgaria, Hungary, and Czechoslovakia. While the merits of the U-2 as a high-altitude reconnaissance platform were thus proven beyond any doubt it also transpired that the aircraft was detected by radar: this dashed any hopes of conducting the overflights without these being observed.

Successful operations over Soviet satellite sates were without doubt valuable: still, it was obvious that the real prize was to obtain photographic intelligence of the Soviet Union itself. However, before such missions could be undertaken two things had to be got out of the way first. One was waiting for the weather over the Soviet Union to improve and the other was that a US Air Force delegation visiting Moscow at that time had to return. Once both conditions were met the first sortie over the USSR – Mission 2013 – was flown by Harvey Stockman on 4 July 1956. The American pilot took his mount over East Germany, across Poland and into Belorussia well past Minsk before heading north to Leningrad (Saint Petersburg), and returning over the Baltic Republics, the Polish coast, and East Germany back to West German airspace. By the next day, on 5 July 1956, Mission 2014 was flown by Carmine Vito who took the U-2 as far as Moscow and beyond – this being the only time the Soviet capital was actually overflown. In addition, three more overflights of the Soviet Union took place, with two of these – Missions 2020 and 2021 – being conducted on the same day, 9 July 1956, while the third, Mission 2023, was flown on 10 July 1956. These overflights covered large areas of Eastern Europe as well as Belorussia, Ukraine and the

The primary 'weapon' of the U-2 was a set of advanced reconnaissance cameras (Hycon Model 732), equipped with lightweight film (specially developed by Kodak for this purpose), and packed into the so-called 'Q-bay' directly behind the cockpit. This photograph was taken during preparations for the first and only sortie that took pilot Carmine Vito directly over Moscow, on 5 July 1956. (USAF)

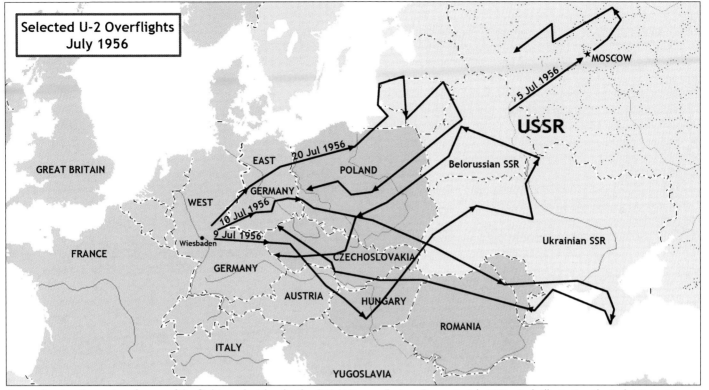

A map showing the routes of some of the flights undertaken by the CIA's U-2s over Eastern Europe in July 1956, nicely illustrating the truly 'strategic' reach of this relatively small aircraft. (Map by Tom Cooper)

Crimean Peninsula in the Soviet Union. While a broken camera shutter ruined much of the photography of one of the missions the remaining two still provided valuable intelligence.

Summarizing the events thus far during the three-week period of 20 June to 10 July 1956, U-2s had flown eight missions including five over the USSR. The said missions yielded a wealth of intelligence information. For example, they dispelled fears that the Soviet Union was building up a fleet of long-range strategic bombers surpassing in numbers their American counterparts of the Strategic Air Command (the so-called 'Bomber Gap'). At the same time advances made by the Soviets in other fields were observed and general information about both their strengths and weaknesses was collected. Still, the overflights were of deep concern for President Eisenhower, who – while aware that they were providing exceptionally valuable intelligence about Soviet capabilities – was also conscious of the fact that they also brought with them the risk of escalating to a war. Therefore, Eisenhower ordered the flights over the Soviet Union to be halted, especially as it was clear that the Soviets were aware of them and made several attempts at intercepting the U-2s. Having stopped their operations over the Eastern Bloc and the Soviet Union the U-2s were tasked with reconnoitring the situation in the Middle East for the time being. Overall, during the first 17 months of their operations, CIA's 'Articles' flew a total of 23 operational missions, including six over the USSR, five over Eastern Europe, and the rest over the Mediterranean. Not one was ever intercepted by any of the dozens (if not hundreds) of interceptors scrambled to catch them.

Soviet Reaction

Moscow was perfectly aware of the overflights, and indeed: it lodged the first related diplomatic protest on 10 July 1956. Similarly, on 16 July the Polish Ambassador to the United States delivered an oral protest concerning overflights of Poland on 20 June and 2 July, which was followed by a protest note from the Czechoslovak Government on 21 July 1956. The Soviets were particularly indignant for they wrongly

believed the overflights were a deliberate provocation taunting them – even more so because the earlier-mentioned US Air Force delegation was shown the newest Soviet fighters and assured in a boastful manner that they could deal with high altitude intrusions into Soviet airspace. Injured pride aside, there were more serious concerns for Moscow. Moreover, if an aircraft was able to penetrate the country's airspace with impunity to make a reconnaissance overflight, it was obvious that such an aircraft could deliver a nuclear attack unopposed. Considering this a pressing question, Nikita Khrushchev – who had meanwhile assumed the posts of the First Secretary of the Communist Party and that of the Prime Minister (Premier) of the USSR – summoned the country's top aviation specialists. In turn, they assured him that such an aircraft must be limited in its payload to reconnaissance equipment and thus would not constitute an immediate physical danger.

Certainly enough, this was of very little satisfaction, and the Soviet government and its armed forces were already attempting to do much more about overflights than sending diplomatic notes and deliberating upon the problem. During the first overflight, on 4 July 1956, U-2 pilot Harvey Stockman reported having seen a number of Soviet fighters unsuccessfully climbing to intercept him. Interestingly, the available Russian sources do not confirm any interception attempt being made that day: it is perfectly possible that the Soviet fighters observed by the American pilots had been engaged in more-or-less routine flying activity. There is however no doubt that an attempted interception did take place on the next day, 5 July. This time, U-2 pilot Carmine Vito sighted five aircraft – including two MiG-19s, two MiG-17s, and a single Yakovlev Yak-25 – attempting to climb towards him.

The next Soviet intercept attempt turned into a farce, as on 6 July 1956 two MiG-19s were scrambled but the ground control guided them against each other – until one of the pilots reported that the 'target' was in fact a friendly aircraft. In retrospect it could be hardly any other way, for as far as it is known no U-2 mission was flown on that day. Yet another interception attempt was made on 9 July 1956 when as many as two U-2 missions were flown over the Soviet Union. At first a single MiG-19 was scrambled – in order to avoid confusion. However shortly after its pilot, Captain Pikalin, engaged the afterburners one of his engines caught fire due to a fuel leak. Fortunately, the fire died out and the pilot managed to safely land his fighter. Undeterred by this mishap the Soviets scrambled three more MiGs but all also failed to intercept either of the U-2s, before one of them ran out of fuel while on return to base. Its pilot, Captain Kapustin, attempted an emergency landing in a nearby field but, alas crashed into an abandoned house. He sustained serious spinal injuries while the aircraft was written off. This was the first, but not last, Soviet loss suffered while attempting to intercept a U-2.[1]

After the initial cessation in the summer of 1956, President Eisenhower was unwilling to approve restarting U-2 missions over the USSR. However, the Hungarian crisis of October–November of the same year, and Eisenhower's re-election by a large margin in early November, encouraged him to authorize renewed missions over the Eastern Bloc, and then also the Soviet Union.

Detachments A, B, and C

By the time overflights were re-launched the U-2-program saw several organisational changes and the involvement of newly-trained personnel – especially pilots. Most notably, the original U-2 unit in West Germany, meanwhile known as Detachment A, was relocated from Wiesbaden to Giebelstadt. Additional units, Detachments B and C, were based at Adana (Incirlik Air Base) in Turkey, and in Japan (Atsugi Air Base), respectively.

The first in the new series of overflights following presidential re-authorisation became Mission 4016, flown on 20 November 1956 by the U-2 piloted by Francis Gary Powers. Taking off from Adana in Turkey he overflew Iran and entered Soviet Airspace over what was then the Soviet Socialist Republic of Armenia. There aerial photographs of Yerevan were taken before an electric malfunction forced Powers to head back to Adana, which he reached without further problems. Additional missions followed, all inciting Soviet protests. A notably strong one was delivered on 15 December 1957 after three US aircraft (paradoxically they were actually Martin RB-57Ds) overflew the Soviet Far East including Vladivostok.

The aforementioned protest resulted in the cessation of direct overflights by the U-2s for the time being. However, reconnaissance flights along the Soviet periphery continued. Of the latter, especially noteworthy was Mission 4019 flown on 22 December 1956, for it was the first operational sortie by a U-2 equipped for electronic intelligence gathering. While direct overflights of Soviet territory were not to be conducted, temporarily as it turned out, operations along the Soviet periphery continued. One such mission on 18 March 1957 involving a U-2 collecting electronic intelligence along the southern border of the USSR resulted in the violation of Soviet airspace due to a compass error compounded by a slight error in the pilot's dead reckoning. Because of heavy cloud cover, the pilot, James W. Cherbonneaux, did not realize he was over the Soviet Union until he saw Soviet fighters attempting to intercept him. However, as in previous such instances the Soviets failed to reach their target.

Finally, despite his reluctance

As of 1956, the MiG-19S was the most advanced supersonic interceptor in service with the V-PVO, and about to enter service with several allied air forces in Eastern Europe. However, with its maximum ceiling of 17,500m (57,400ft), it proved unable to catch any of the U-2s. This experience prompted work on the development of high-altitude variants with larger wings and rocket boosters, expected to reach altitudes of up to 19,100m (62,700ft). Eventually, all such efforts were abandoned. (Albert Grandolini Collection)

Francis Gary Powers posing for a photo with Clarence L Kelly Johnson, designer of the U-2, in front of one of the CIA-operated examples. (CIA)

concerning this matter, President Eisenhower was persuaded to re-authorise direct overflights of Soviet territory which he did on 6 May 1957. Meanwhile, work was underway to make the U-2 less detectable by radar: early measures in this regard all failed to bring the desired results. Of greater practical value was the fitting of improved engines which increased the U-2's maximum altitude to 74,600 feet (22,700 meters). Furthermore, new locations were added for the conduct of operations, including Eielson Air Force Base (AFB) in Alaska and Lahore in Pakistan. On 8 June 1957, a U-2 took off from Eielson to conduct the first intentional overflight of the Soviet Union since President Eisenhower gave his renewed approval.

Missions were also flown from Pakistan with one conducted on 5 August 1957 yielding an important find. Namely the U-2 piloted by Buster Edens photographed the Tyratam (Baikonur) missile and space test centre. It is interesting to note that this important discovery was made after the pilot chose to fly along a railroad track to find where it led; for it must be added that despite careful mission planning the man in the cockpit was not left without initiative.

A number of other flights took place resulting in valuable intelligence being gathered. As it retrospectively transpired, those missions flown in August 1957 represented the 'high water mark' of U-2 overflights of the USSR.

Soviet All Out-Effort

The U-2 missions described thus far were taking place against a background of failed Soviet efforts to stop them. Having received reports about the less than successful attempts to put an end to American high-altitude reconnaissance overflights the Soviet leader Nikita Khrushchev announced that any pilot who could shoot down such an intruding aircraft was to receive the Hero of the Soviet Union title, promotion and a substantial material reward. But all incentives combined could not help the fact that the Soviet fighter aircraft in service at that time were unable to reach the altitude at which the U-2 operated. However, new fighter-interceptor types were about to be added into Soviet inventory. Moreover, the Soviets would also soon have a sufficient number of surface-to-air missiles to facilitate an effective defence of a number of important facilities. The locations in question were all of obvious interest to US intelligence and thus likely to be 'visited' by a U-2. As a matter of fact, during the 5 July 1956 mission, when the U-2 piloted by Carmine Vito overflew Moscow, among other things photographs were taken of the S-25 (SA-1) SAM sites being set up to defend the Soviet capital. However, at that time they were not combat ready: no other US reconnaissance aircraft ever reappeared over Moscow. That said, the S-75 (SA-2) missile system entered service in 1957 and SAM sites were being set up around a number of locations in the Soviet Union. Moreover, the first SAM-sites were also provided to several close allies. The S-75 was thus to soon prove its worth.

3
EARLY SAM SUCCESS

Before continuing to relate the history of high-altitude overflights of the Soviet Union it is fitting at this point to describe the early combat use of the weapon system which would become the U-2's nemesis. As mentioned earlier, by the late 1950s the S-25 and the SA-75 surface-to-air missiles systems had already entered service but were initially available only in limited numbers – and operated by SAM sites defending only the most important locations in the USSR, such as Moscow, Leningrad, Sverdlovsk (Yekaterinburg), and a handful of others. While the Soviet airspace was not safe from penetrations by high-altitude reconnaissance aircraft a country featuring prominently in Soviet plans was having the same problem: this was the People's Republic of China.[1]

Looking beyond the Bamboo Curtain

Since 1949 when the Chinese Communist forces expelled the Chinese Nationalist forces from mainland China to the island of Taiwan, the US and allied ability to monitor the developments taking place on the mainland of China was drastically reduced. However, because of the People's Republic of China's (PRC) significance and potential, and its close alliance with the Soviet Union, Washington and Langley considered it 'vitally important' to keep an eye on the events there. Considering this situation, reconnaissance aircraft were the best – and, sometimes the only – means for the USA to obtain the authoritative information sought. Thus, it can be concluded that the reasons for aerial reconnaissance of the PRC were in essence the same as for the overflights of the USSR.

Before long, the skies of the PRC were frequented by a number of uninvited aerial 'visitors', ranging from RAF Spitfires flying out of Hong Kong, to diverse transports and reconnaissance jets of what became the Republic of China Air Force (ROCAF), to U-2s that made a number of overflights starting in May 1957. These flights were usually launched from Peshawar airfield in northern Pakistan. Naturally, the Chinese detected the incursions and undertook measures to confront the intruders: however, while regularly successful against low-flying nocturnal incursions by slow ROCAF aircraft, they experienced significant problems with intercepting high-flying reconnaissance

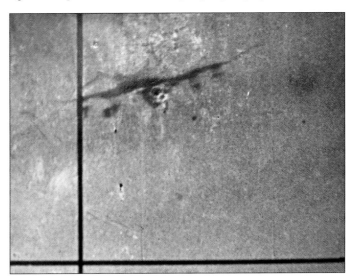

A still from a gun-camera film of one of two PLAAF interceptors, taken during the interception of a ROCAF RB-57A over Shandong, on 18 February 1958. (Albert Grandolini Collection)

Two MiG-17Fs of the PLAAF as seen while powering their engines prior to take-off. With its service ceiling of 16,600m (54,500ft), the type – which entered operational service in China in early 1958 – proved capable of catching one of the ROCAF's RB-57As that had descended for unknown reasons, but could not reach the U-2. (Via Tom Cooper))

aircraft. It was only on 18 February 1958, that a Taiwanese-operated RB-57A fell victim to two MiG-15bis or MiG-17F interceptors of the People's Liberation Army Naval Air Force (PLANAF), over Shandong.[2]

Early on, the inability of the armed forces of the PRC to effectively combat such targets was hardly surprising. Not only the PLANAF, but especially the People's Liberation Army Air Force (PLAAF) – the air force of Communist China – was almost exclusively equipped with the same Soviet-made interceptors, such as the MiG-15 and MiG-17, which had already failed to catch the CIA's U-2s overflying Eastern Europe. Therefore, high-altitude reconnaissance aircraft provided by the USA to the Taiwanese initially proved capable of roaming over mainland China with impunity.

Project Diamond Lil

The first advanced type capable of operating at high altitudes to enter service with the ROCAF became the RB-57D. After a number of pilots from No. 4 Squadron were trained to fly it, three such aircraft were supplied by the CIA within the frame of Project Diamond Lil in 1958. Starting in early 1959, they began undertaking deep penetrations of the PRC's airspace, usually at altitudes of 20,000m (65,616ft) or more. Unsurprisingly, they promptly proved to be operating out of the

reach of the PLAAF's and the PLANAF's interceptors, not to mention traditional anti-aircraft artillery. However, nothing lasts forever, and the 'Reds' were about to come up with a worthy answer to the challenge. The Communist leaders in Beijing requested assistance from Moscow: the Soviets responded quickly, and in late 1958 and early 1959, delivered the first out of a total of five SA-75 Dvina SAM-systems, and one training set, together with 62 V-750 (1D) and V-750V (11D) missiles, and all the necessary support equipment.[3]

Considering that the Soviets were themselves having a problem with Western high-altitude reconnaissance aircraft penetrating their airspace the very fact that as many as five surface-to-air missile batteries were supplied to the People's Republic of China clearly shows the importance that the Soviets attached to their Asian ally. The hardware was accompanied by Colonel Victor Slusar, who headed a team of specialists (among them Lieutenant-Colonel Aleksander Piecko, Lieutenant-Colonel Yuriy Galkin and others) tasked with training PLA personnel on the new weapon system. Wasting little time, they got down to work. Soviet instructors noted that the Chinese trainees showed a great desire to acquire knowledge and were learning quickly. As a result, it was possible to conduct the first live firing exercise on 19 April 1959 in the Gobi desert, when radar reflectors suspended under

One of three RB-57Ds provided by the CIA to the ROCAF within the framework of Project Diamond Lil in 1958. This jet wore the serial 33981 on the fin, and the ROCAF registration 5644 on the rear fuselage (for further details, see colour section), while retaining the camouflage pattern applied by the USAF. (Albert Grandolini Collection)

Jack in the Box

The CIA's decision to deliver RB-57s and then U-2s to the ROCAF came not out of the blue: its origins can be traced back to the 1940s, when the USA were supporting the Chinese Nationalists in their struggle against Imperial Japan, and then the Chinese Communists. In 1949-1950, the Communists won the Chinese Civil War, forcing the Nationalist government and much of its armed forces to withdraw to the island of Formosa (to use the Portuguese name) or Taiwan (its Chinese name). While the Communists proclaimed the People's Republic of China (PRC) in 1950, the Nationalists established the Republic of China (ROC): the latter was granted a seat at the United Nations, and was considered the official government of China by the USA and allies.

Of course, the leadership in Beijing was keen to destroy the 'rebels' on Taiwan and began planning an invasion of the island shortly after taking over on the mainland. The Korean War postponed the related designs for at least three years, but also bought time for the PRC to establish and build-up a large air force, much of which was combat-tested. Between 1954 and 1957, the Communist armed forces – consisting of the PLA, PLAAF, and the People's Liberation Army Navy (PLAN) – secured a number of Nationalist-controlled islands along the coast. In turn, and with US support, the ROCAF ran near-constant reconnaissance operations and the infiltration of agents over mainland China – with nearly a dozen such missions shot down in the 1950s. In summer 1958, the PLA set in motion preparations to assault the last two Nationalist-controlled islands off the coast, Matsu and Quemoy. The priority in any such operation was to secure air superiority, which in turn would enable the PLA to isolate the local garrisons, then subject them to intense bombardment, and thus 'soften' them prior to an amphibious assault. Correspondingly, the PLAAF deployed over 600 combat aircraft, including its brand-new MiG-17F interceptors, to air bases opposite Taiwan.

The ROCAF responded by using its North American F-86F Sabre interceptors to fly near-constant combat air patrols not only over Matsu and Quemoy, but along the coast of the PRC, and with the vigerous activity of all available reconnaissance aircraft. Moreover, alerted to Beijing's intentions, Washington reacted by deploying six carrier battle groups of the US Navy into the waters around Taiwan, a squadron each of Lockheed F-104A Starfighter and North American F-100D Super Sabres, plus a full wing of McDonnell F-101C Voodoo interceptors, on the island. Together with a squadron of Douglas F4D-1 Skyray interceptors of the US Marine Corps, these freed the ROCAF's interceptors for operations over Matsu and Quemoy.

The resulting Third Taiwan Strait Crisis culminated in a series of at least 13 massive air combats fought over the Straits of Taiwan between late July and late September 1958. According to official releases from both sides, the ROCAF claimed to have shot down 31 or 32 aircraft wearing the Red Stars while losing three of their own; in turn, the PLAAF claimed to have shot down 14 Taiwanese jets while losing five of their own. Whatever the outcome of the air combats was, one fact was sure: the PLAAF failed to secure aerial superiority over the two islands, and the PLA was forced to abandon its plan to invade them.

Ironically, the Taiwan Strait Crisis had far-reaching consequences in so far as it helped the Communists – not only in the PRC, but in the USSR, too – to narrow down the constantly growing gap in high technologies. During this affair, Washington ordered a team of two pilots and three engineers of the US Marine Corps, together with a batch of 40 GAR-9 guided air-to-air missiles – re-designated to AIM-9B Sidewinder in 1962 – to Taiwan. Working under conditions of utmost secrecy, they installed this brand-new weapon on about a dozen F-86Fs. On 24 September, 1958, ROCAF Sabres clashed with PLAAF MiGs again, and claimed nine 'confirmed' and two 'probable' kills, in exchange for one loss of their own: three or four of the MiGs may have been shot down by the brand-new air-to-air missiles in their first ever operational use. Indeed, the Sidewinder proved a major surprise for the Communist pilots because it enabled the Taiwanese Sabres to shoot down MiG-17Fs even when these were underway at their maximum operational altitude, which was about 5,000ft (1,524m) higher than that of the F-86s.

Overall, pilots of the ROCAF fired six GAR-9s to claim a total of four 'kills' during the Crisis. Indeed, one of two Sidewinders that failed to bring down its target had actually also scored a hit: however, it failed to detonate after embedding itself inside the fuselage of a PLAAF MiG-17F. The aircraft made a safe landing, the missile was extracted, and the Communists promptly rushed it to the USSR, where the weapon was carefully taken apart and then reverse-engineered, bit by bit.

Thus came into being the R-3S (ASCC/NATO-codename 'AA-2 Atoll'), the most widely deployed air-to-air missile in Soviet and (mainland) Chinese service of the following decade, and the primary weapon of an entirely new 'U-2-Hunter' that was to emerge in the early 1960s: the MiG-21.

A GAR-9 (future AIM-9B Sidewinder), as seen installed on an improvised inboard underwing hardpoint of a ROCAF F-86F in 1958. (USMC)

R-3S missile, as seen installed on its launch rail underneath the left wing of a MiG-21F-13. (Photo by Sean O'Connor)

One of the V-750V missiles provided to the PLA by the Soviets, seen on its PR-11 transloader. (Chinese Internet)

A pair of PLA-operated V-750V missiles in position on their SM-63-1 launchers. (via Tom Cooper)

aircraft. Moreover, it took great care to retain the moment of surprise. Correspondingly, all the related deployments and redeployments were handled in a particularly secretive manner, with the personnel pretending to be drilling-crews looking for natural resources with their 'complex technical equipment'.

The First SAM-Kill

Regardless of how eager the PLA's SAM-operators were to prove their skills, nothing happened. For two weeks after their deployment outside Beijing, not a single overflight took place. Indeed, nothing happened even during the most-tense period of 1959 – the celebrations marking the 10th anniversary of the People's Republic of China, between 1 and 4 October, when it was thought that Taiwan was likely to make a provocative aerial incursion. No unwelcome "guest" from across the Straits of Formosa appeared. Then, on the morning of 5 October 1959, an aircraft flying from the direction of Taiwan entered PRC airspace over Fujian province. The PLAAF's radars tracked the intruder as it flew in the direction of Nanking, and interceptors were scrambled. However, because the RB-57D maintained an altitude of 20,000-21,000 meters they were unable to intercept. Meanwhile the airspace violator crossed the Yangtse River and came within about 500km of Beijing. For a while, it appeared the hour of the SAMs was near, when – all of a sudden – the Taiwanese turned in the direction of Shanghai, and flew away, never approaching within range of the SA-75s. The Chinese were not only disappointed but above all very worried that their SAMs were somehow exposed. However, after some deliberation they decided not to make any hasty moves but to wait for another chance – and as subsequent events showed it was the right decision.

Two days later, on 7 October 1959, in an almost exact repetition of the previous event, the Chinese radar operators detected a high-altitude aerial intruder. Because of the obvious importance of the events unfolding the efforts to deal with the airspace violator were coordinated by the general staff of the PLA with Colonel Slusar present to lend advice should it become necessary. Even though experience had so far demonstrated that manned interceptors were unable to catch an RB-57D, they were ordered into the air and took up the chase hoping that the reconnaissance aircraft might lose altitude because of a malfunction or for some other reason. Meanwhile the intruder, which was indeed an RB-57D (ROCAF serial 5643, US FY serial 53-3978) – piloted by Captain Ying Chin Wong – continued to

parachutes dropped by aircraft were used as simulated targets. Once the latter flew away the former were successfully engaged. Although the PLA's personnel learned fast, it still had to come to grips with a wide range of complex technical issues and thus it took them a few months longer before the Soviets judged the Chinese as 'fit' to utilise their new weapon system in combat.

The 1st Surface-to-Air Guided Missile Battalion of the PLA was declared operational on 20 September 1959, closely followed by the 2nd Surface-to-Air Guided Missile Battalion. Right from the start, both units were entirely manned by the Chinese, without any kind of Soviet assistance. Of course, they were not entirely on their own: Colonel Slusar remained in the PRC as an advisor, but all the other Soviets were withdrawn. This was to prove a wise choice, not only because Slusar had trained the Chinese SAM-operators, but also had established a good rapport with them in the process. Still, the following 'show' was to be entirely run by the Chinese, and the Soviet advisor played no important role in the events.

The first two PLA SAM-units became operational at the time that the aerial incursions by the RB-57Ds of No. 4 Squadron ROCAF were overflying even Beijing in June of 1959. Working methodically, the PLA positioned its few SAM-sites in the vicinity of the Chinese capital, so as to cover the most likely routes used by the Taiwanese reconnaissance

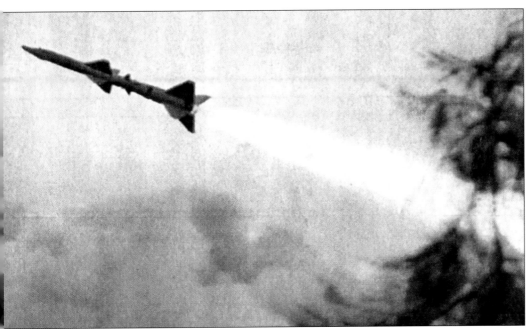

A Chinese-operated V-750 missile of the S-75 system, seen only a second after leaving the SM-63-I launcher. (via Tom Cooper)

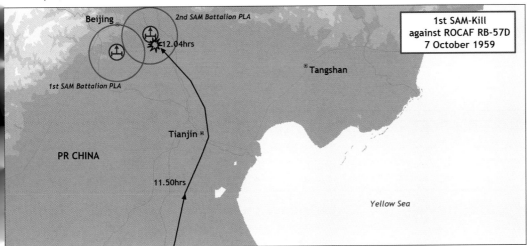

A map reconstructing the last 15 minutes of Captain Wong's flight with the RB-57D towards Beijing, where he was shot down by S-75s fired by Yue Zhenhua's 2nd Surface-to-Air Guided Missile Battalion of the PLA on 7 October 1959. (Map by Tom Cooper)

the pieces of wreckage that were collected: it was unsurprising that the reconnaissance aircraft fell apart. Unfortunately, the incident also proved fatal for the Taiwanese pilot.

A Secret well kept

Indeed, Captain Wong seems to have been killed or at least badly injured by the detonation of the first V-750, as he did not manage to transmit a radio message informing his home-base about the disaster that befell him. Of course, ROCAF's RB-57D pilots were supposed to maintain radio silence during their forays deep over the PRC, but such a catastrophic event as being shot down would surely have been a reason to ignore related orders and report. However, because Wong failed to report anything before disappearing, Beijing released no reports about the shoot-down, and because Taipei expected that the 'Reds' would explode with propaganda about such an achievement, all the Taiwanese knew was that one of their aircraft had gone missing. Indeed, the ROCAF remained convinced that the PRC still lacked the means necessary to shoot down an aircraft flying as high as their RB-57Ds did. Therefore, they drew the logical conclusion that Wong's aircraft

fly in the direction of Beijing and this time it did not turn away. Soon it became clear that the Taiwanese aircraft would come into range of the SAMs and for this reason the manned interceptors were ordered to disengage thus clearing the sky for the missiles.

The RB-57D was on a course that would take it into the range of the 2nd Surface-to-Air Guided Missile Battalion, commanded by Yue Zhenhua. As the distance dropped to 200km he received the order to destroy the reconnaissance aircraft. The battalion's radars picked up the target from a range of 115 km: the range was dropping rapidly, and when it decreased to 41km Yue Zhenhua gave the command to launch a salvo of three missiles. The first V-750 lifted off at 12:04hrs, soon followed by two more. About 40 seconds later, as the target was at a distance of 29-30km, the first of them scored a hit: the target changed course and began rapidly losing altitude. When it was down to about 5,000 metres, it disappeared from the radar screens, and was correctly assessed as 'disintegrated'. The destruction of the RB-57D was promptly reported up the chain of command of the PLA, and the General Staff officers – accompanied by Slusar – soon arrived on the scene with help of a helicopter. The remains of the downed aircraft were strewn over a radius of 5,000 to 6,000 metres and identified as those of an RB-57D. As many as 2,471 shrapnel holes were found in

Yue Zhenhua, commander of the 2nd Surface-to-Air Guided Missile Battalion of the PLA – the first unit to score a hit against a manned, high-altitude reconnaissance aircraft using a surface-to-air missile. Zhenhua went on to score multiple additional such kills. (via Tom Cooper)

must have crashed into the South China Sea as a result of some kind of technical mishap. This was also what the official statement for the press cited – which in turn was exactly what the leaders in Beijing were waiting for: soon, the PRC reacted by issuing its own statement, stressing that the missing aircraft was shot down, and that the other side had an 'obvious problem with facts'. That said, the Communists did take care to leave out one crucial detail: the means by which the RB-57D was shot down. Thus, not only the presence, but also the actual capability of the brand-new Soviet SAM-system were to remain an enigma for the West for half a year longer.

In fact, the method by which Wong's RB-57 was shot down was to remain a big secret for another 25 years. Even then, very few outside of the PRC paid attention. Such secrecy stemmed from the fact that when the SAMs were first delivered to the Chinese, Beijing and Moscow agreed that if a foreign aircraft were to be shot down, then both sides would abstain from releasing any significant details – especially any kind of information concerning the use of surface-to-air missiles. Initially, it was considered sensible not to reveal the capabilities of the new weapon. However, later on, it was little more than a very general military secrecy that prevented any related releases: as is now well-known, and mildly expressed, this was not always perfectly logical in communist-ruled countries.[4]

Since the surface-to-air missiles themselves, as well as the training necessary to effectively utilise them, were both provided to China by the Soviets the shooting down of the RB-57D on 7 October 1959 can reasonably be labelled a 'Soviet SAM success', or at least a 'success of a Soviet SAM', although the system was entirely Chinese manned. On the contrary, the first Soviet SAM-kill was to take place barely a month later: on 16 November 1959, the V-PVO deployed its SA-75s to shoot down the US-made WS-416L spy blimp floating at an altitude of 24,000m above the city of Volgograd (formerly Stalingrad). Sadly, most of the details about this engagement are lacking, except for one point contrary to what many Russian-language reports cite, the aerostat in question was not hit while underway at an altitude of 28,000 metres (78,740ft) – which would have been outside the reach of the S-75. Obviously, the destruction of a spy blimp was not considered as great a feat as the downing of a high-altitude reconnaissance aircraft, even though there was nothing demeaning about it. The Soviets had to wait for only a few months longer before achieving this too.

4
U-2 MISSIONS CONTINUE

Meanwhile aerial reconnaissance of the Soviet Union continued. It took the form of peripheral flights which seldom crossed into Soviet airspace if at all, as well as direct overflights of Soviet territory. The U-2s were utilised in both types of operations and was the only type used in the latter. Having reached their high watermark in August 1957, U-2 overflights of the Soviet Union subsequently decreased in number. Still, four more missions penetrating deep into Soviet airspace took place in the September – October 1957 time period but from then onwards they would become truly singular events. Only one such mission was conducted in 1958 when on 1 March that year a U-2 overflew the Soviet Far East. The aircraft used employed measures which were supposed to hide it from radar detection, but a Soviet protest delivered a few days after the overflight demonstrated that the U-2 was detected and tracked. In view of the situation on 7 March 1958 President Eisenhower ordered an immediate cessation of missions over the Soviet Union. This was to remain in effect till the summer of 1959.[1]

President Eisenhower had numerous reasons to curtail aerial reconnaissance activity. He not only desired that the United States avoid being perceived as truculent or provocative for the sake of domestic as well as world opinion but also to be able to push through a number of arms-limitation and confidence-building proposals which, if they were to be effective, needed Soviet cooperation. Such was obviously impossible to secure as long as Soviet airspace was being violated. The United States may have had genuine concerns about the Soviet threat, but in protesting against such airspace violations as high-altitude reconnaissance flights the Soviets were in the right. Last-but-not-least, what such missions were conducted for, if not preparation for attack, was also a legitimate question. Further, President Eisenhower was being assured that such overflights as those made by the U-2s were as good as undetectable, yet it consistently proved to be otherwise. To add insult to injury President Eisenhower was also deceived by his own military and intelligence communities about the use of aerostats and found himself confronted with diplomatic protests as well as embarrassing displays of American balloons which had gone down over the Soviet Union. Prestige aside, Cold War "games" sometimes turned deadly serious, a case in point being when on 2 September 1958 an American C-130 strayed into Soviet Armenia and was shot down with the loss of seventeen lives. Without further elaborating it is sufficient to say that the American president had ample reasons when he decided to stop US aerial reconnaissance activity over the Soviet Union.

Back Over the USSR

While the U-2s were not left unemployed – they were the primary US reconnaissance platform during the Lebanon Crisis of 1958 – it took considerable time before they returned to the skies over the Soviet Union. President Eisenhower was prompted to re-authorize overflights of Soviet territory by a number of real achievements as well as boastful claims made by the Soviets in the field of missile technology. In early 1959 concerns arose in the United States that the Soviet missile arsenal would numerically eclipse that of the Americans – the so-called missile gap. Initially the US president resisted calls for renewed overflights of the Soviet Union. Progress was being made on US reconnaissance satellites which in a few years were to reach a level of technical maturity that would allow their practical use and thus make manned overflights by reconnaissance aircraft such as the U-2 redundant. It was also clear that because of the sheer amount of resources and work needed the Soviet Union would not be realistically able to build up a massive intercontinental ballistic missile force in the meantime. Additionally, in view of the political damage to the United Sates should a U-2 go down over the Soviet Union for whatever reason, undertaking a reconnaissance mission seemed to not be worth the risk.

The rationale laid out meant that only flights along the Soviet periphery and without penetrating the country's airspace were authorized. While these produced interesting results they could not substitute for the direct reconnoitring of Soviet missile facilities. Thus, despite good reasons to abstain, voices from within the Defense Department arguing to renew overflights of the Soviet Union mounted. Finally, the US president was convinced and approved a single overflight which took place on 9 July 1959. During the said mission photographs of Tyratam (Baikonur) were taken and yielded valuable intelligence information. A second mission in 1959 was flown on 6 December that year. It was noteworthy for the fact that British pilot Squadron

By the time they returned over the USSR in 1959-1960, most of the CIA-operated U-2As were modified to the U-2C standard through the installation of more powerful engines (necessitating slightly wider intakes), underwing slipper tanks, and 'canoe' fairings of various lengths added to the top fuselage. Moreover, they were all painted a sea blue colour overall (see colour section for details).

Leader Robert Robinson was behind the U-2's controls. It was the first overflight of Soviet Territory by a U-2 with a British pilot in the cockpit – though British pilots had already flown the aircraft on missions elsewhere – requiring the approval of the United Kingdom's prime minister. Good photographic material was brought back from the mission, however no new information regarding Soviet missile developments was obtained because work in this field was being conducted at locations not overflown on that occasion.

Finally Sighted

So far, the Soviets were unable to effectively oppose U-2 overflights even though they were able to detect and track them. It is also not clear how much they knew about the elusive airspace violator. The Soviet military intelligence officer Pyotr Semyonovich Popov, who offered his services to the Americans, informed his handler in 1958 that the Soviets were in possession of 'full technical details' on the U-2. The accuracy of this claim remains hard to judge until this day. What is beyond dispute is that despite a number of attempts being undertaken by Soviet fighters they did not even come close to intercepting the U-2. It appears the Soviets did not even know what type of aircraft they were dealing with for the mysterious air space violator remained an "intruder" or "target" – a blip on the radar screen which nobody

even saw. While this hardly confirms any claims of having precise intelligence about the U-2 it also does not fully disprove them. Unless some important detailed information was obtained which could be used to bring the aircraft down there was no point in acquainting interceptor pilots or anybody else within the PVO with such intelligence because this could have compromised the source.

Possibly the first Soviet to actually gain visual contact with the U-2 was a pilot from one of the units assigned to the Turkestan Military District. In February 1959 a MiG-19 was scrambled to intercept a high-flying intruder which entered Soviet air space from the south. Using the afterburner, the MiG managed to reach its maximum operational ceiling of 17,500m (54,414ft). The foreign aircraft was still about 3,000m higher and thus out of reach, but close enough for the Soviet pilot to actually see it. Upon returning back to base the pilot gave a detailed account of the event and also made a sketch showing an aircraft with a slim fuselage and long wings. Considering the circumstances, this was a fairly accurate description. The report was sent up all the way to Moscow and generated enough interest for a special commission to come down from the Soviet capital and investigate the events at the scene. Yet the commission failed to take the matter seriously, concluding that the pilot involved made the story up in order to draw attention and receive a reward. While that

An unknown MiG-19 pilot of the V-PVO was the first Soviet citizen to actually see a U-2 underway high over the southern USSR in February 1959. This photograph shows one of the early MiG-19Ps, the first radar-equipped variant developed as an all-weather and night-interceptor for the V-PVO. (USAF)

story sounds plausible it has one major weakness – namely as far as it is known no U-2 overflight took place in February 1959 with, as described above, the only two flights over the Soviet Union being conducted on 19 July and 6 December that year.

Whatever the case, the U-2 was exposed by accident, which is not an infrequent occurrence with many other secrets also being revealed by chance. It so happened that on 24 September 1959 a U-2 made an emergency landing, due to engine problems, at a civilian airfield used by a glider club in Japan. The aircraft and pilot were quickly secured and then moved away by the Americans, but the story made it to the press and appeared in Japanese newspapers the next day. Articles published described an aircraft which if to go by its layout was best suited for high-altitude flying; it also noted a window for cameras thus hinting that it probably had a reconnaissance role. Thus, regardless of any intelligence or lack thereof, the U-2 was – finally – revealed to the Soviets. Of course, this fact alone was still far from granting them the capability of stopping the overflights.

Getting Closer

The first U-2 mission in 1960 took place on 5 February that year. As with the last overflight in 1959 this time the pilot was also British – Squadron Leader John MacArthur sat in the U-2's cockpit. The mission was successful in that it brought back high-quality photographic images allowing analysts to make a number of valuable observations. For example, a new bomber prototype was spotted on the Kazan airfield, while no new missiles sites were discovered.

As in previous cases, the Soviets proved unable to effectively challenge the high-flying aircraft. Having said that, it has to be noted that by 1960 the Soviet arsenal was augmented by a number of new weapon systems. Among them were MiG-21F-13 and Sukhoi Su-9 interceptors. While the former was for the most part assigned to the Frontal Aviation the latter strengthened PVO units. The MiG-21F-13 lacked the radar but was armed with a single 30mm cannon and a pair of R-3S air-to-air missiles (ASCC/NATO-codename 'AA-2 Atoll'). The Su-9 was an even more powerful, high flying and fast interceptor fitted with an on-board radar. In theory it should have been capable of reaching a maximum flight altitude of 20,000m (66,000ft), and shooting down a U-2 with the help of up to four K-5/RS-1U (ASCC/NATO-codename 'AA-1 Alkali') air-to-air missiles. However, introducing a radically new combat aircraft into service generated a number of problems. The pilots had to gain experience in both flying new aircraft as well as operating their weapon systems and electronics – although Su-9-pilots, for example, never fired a single air-to-air missile in training. Similarly, ground control personnel had to learn how to utilize new capabilities of the aircraft they maintained, and – foremost – ground-controllers had to learn how to bring them into a position from which they could successfully engage. Finally, the introduction to service of such a complex aircraft as the Su-9 also presented a great challenge to the ground crews. One should also keep in mind that re-equipping entire units took considerable time and in 1960 most of the aircraft defending the Soviet Union were still first-generation MiG and Yak fighters: Su-9s were still available only in small numbers. There was hardly a single interceptor wing with a squadron including more than, literally, a handful of aircraft.

On the contrary, the SAM-systems were now reasonably well-deployed. While Moscow was defended by the massive S-25, S-75s were in position around Leningrad (St. Petersburg), Sverdlovsk (Ekaterinburg), Baku, and some other locations. The only issue now was for the Soviet air defences to finally catch one of the intruders.

The MiG-21F-13 was in the process of entering service with selected units of the Soviet Air Force in 1960. Officially having a service ceiling of 17,500m (57,400ft), it was actually flight-tested up to nearly 20,000m (66,000ft). Moreover, by 1961 it was to receive advanced armament in the form of two R-3S infra-red homing missiles – reverse engineered from the GAR-9/AIM-9B Sidewinder 'captured' during the Taiwan Strait Crisis of 1958. (USAF)

Operation Square Deal: The Longest Hunt

On 9 April 1960, a CIA-operated U-2A flown by Bob Ericson penetrated the airspace over the southern USSR. Run within the framework of Operation Square Deal, this overflight saw Ericson gliding all the way to the Semipalatinsk nuclear test site, before returning to make multiple overflights of the Sary-Shagan missile range (10th State Research and Testing Site), and the Tyratam (Baikonour) rocket test site – to mention only the most important installations. Unsurprisingly, the entire PVO apparatus sprang into life, launching feverish attempts to intercept the intruder. While

Of a design similar to that of the MiG-21, but much bigger and more powerful, was another new interceptor in the process of entering service with the V-PVO as of 1960: the Su-9. Equipped with radar and RS-2U air-to-air missiles (four of which are visible in this photograph), and with a maximum ceiling of 20,000m (66,000ft), it was expected to become capable of reliably intercepting U-2s. (USAF)

A launch ramp for the Soviet R-7 Semyorka intercontinental ballistic missile (ASCC/NATO-codename 'SS-6 Sapwood'), at Tyuratam, as photographed by Ericson. Overflights like his on 9 April 1960, had shown to the Americans, that – while a relatively powerful missile – the R-7 project was actually heading nowhere, and that the USSR was lagging behind even in this field. Certainly enough, Moscow then exploited the R-7 for propaganda purposes – foremost to fire the first man into space. (CIA)

Kharabad, Kokayty and Chirchik. Deeper over the USSR, there was only the 678th Guards Mixed Test Air Regiment of the 60th Mixed Test Aviation Division: this Kambala AB-based unit was serving testing purposes, but was also for the protection of Sary Shagan, and had at least a handful of Su-9s assigned. While – as so many times before and after – all the intercept attempts by older MiG-17s and MiG-19s failed, the Su-9 piloted by Captain Doroshenko managed to climb high enough to actually report a visual contact with the target. Fortunately for Ericson, Doroshenko was unable to maintain altitude and forced to descend before he could initiate an engagement with air-to-air missiles.

Moreover, the U-2 not only managed to escape unscathed, but the Soviets also lost one of their interceptors. For unknown reasons, one of the MiG-19s involved in the pursuit found itself in trouble. Senior Lieutenant Vladimir Karchevski ejected just before his aircraft crashed: tragically, he was already very low and his parachute failed to open properly, and thus the pilot was killed. Circumstances of this accident were never sufficiently determined, but probably related to fuel starvation: the Soviet hunt for the U-2 thus claimed its first fatality.[2]

Khrushchev in his memoires states that SAMs were deployed to protect most of the facilities in question, this might well be a mistake on his part. Actually, the Turkestan Military District – the top command responsible for the defence of the USSR along the borders with Iran, Afghanistan, and the PRC – had relatively little on hand to act immediately. Foremost were the units of the 49th Tactical Air Army equipped with MiG-17s and MiG-19s, and based at Kzyl-Arvat,

When Khrushchev learned of yet another unsuccessful attempt to stop the American high-altitude overflights he was furious. There were no 'heads rolling' – at least not in the literal sense – but a number of officers were penalised. It was obvious that the Soviet leader would not tolerate another failure.

5

MAYDAY MAYHEM – THE DOWNING OF F. G. POWERS

The Americans were determined to collect as much intelligence of value as possible on Soviet nuclear missile development and everything else. Thus, even before the 9 April overflight another mission was already authorized by the US president – even though not without an important condition. Namely it was his firm wish that the overflight be conducted before 1 May 1960. This was so because a summit of the leaders of the United State, the Soviet Union, Great Britain and France was planned to take place in Paris on 17 May 1960. The 9 April overflight did not result in a Soviet note of protest and if another successful intelligence gathering mission took place more than two weeks before the scheduled top-level meeting it was reasonable to believe that it would not affect the political climate at the summit which was of importance if the coming together of leaders was to produce any positive results.[1]

Gearing up

Before relating what was to become the last-ever U-2 flight over the Soviet Union, a number of issues deserve to be raised. The mission in question – codenamed OPERATION GRAND SLAM – was planned to be like no other before: at earlier times, the U-2s would penetrate the Soviet Union's airspace for a few hours, before returning almost in the same direction from which they came. In this case, the mission was to cross over the entire USSR, from the border with Afghanistan in the south, to the border with Norway and Sweden, in the north. Coded Mission 4154, this was to become the 24th overflight of the Soviet Union. Naturally an experienced pilot was selected to fly it and the man chosen was Francis Gary Powers. Another important point was the perception of how vulnerable the U-2 was by that time and gauging the risk associated with the planned operation. While it appears that the Americans were oblivious to the fact that on 9 April the U-2 escaped only because the Soviet pilot flying the pursuing Su-9 interceptor lacked experience in handling his aircraft at a high altitude, they had a general idea of the mounting hazards that the overflights were facing. The Soviet ability to detect and track the aircraft as well as some of the attempts at interception by manned fighters were noted. Moreover, the SAM-threat was taken into consideration – although not sufficiently, as it was about to transpire. The flight path of each U-2 mission over the Soviet Union was planned in such a manner as to avoid known SAM sites. One of the locations to be overflown in the course of Powers' mission was Sverdlovsk which was defended by SAMs: this fact became known to US intelligence because the S-75 sites were photographed during vice-president Richard Nixon's visit to the USSR in 1959. It was a major internal failure within the CIA not to pass this vital piece of information to those involved in the U-2's mission planning. Even so, it is still hard to avoid the conclusion that the Americans considered their high-flying jet to be capable of operating beyond the reach of what was its primary adversary: this can only be explained by earlier Soviet failures to bring down any of the U-2s. The supposed impunity was about to end in a particularly dramatic fashion.

Eisenhower's permission was also influenced by other political considerations. The overflight was to take place shortly before 1 May 1960 – International Workers' Day – and the Union of the Soviet Socialist Republics was a self-proclaimed champion of the working class, and thus celebrated this as one of its major public holidays, including running a massive parade at Moscow's Red Square. An overflight on such a day had to be expected to be understood by Moscow as a particularly blatant provocation: the president of the USA did not consider it as such, although extremely cautious about his political planning.

For a number of reasons, including the weather and aircraft availability amongst others, it proved difficult to meet the presidential deadline. Finally, literally at the last moment, in late April, the aircraft to be used in the mission, the U-2C Article 360 (US FY serial 56-6693) arrived at Peshawar airfield in northern Pakistan, on 30 April. With everything in place, Francis Gary Powers took his place in the cockpit before dawn of 1 May 1960. Now only the coded "go ahead" for the mission had to arrive from Washington. After extensive difficulties with radio communications (a bad omen for anybody who is superstitious), this was received: Powers took off and turned towards the north-west, taking a course over Afghanistan before entering Soviet airspace.

The Hunt is on

The Soviets detected the intruding aircraft as early as 05:36hrs local time in the morning. By 06:00hrs the HQ and the main air defence post of the V-PVO in Moscow took over the coordination of efforts aimed at intercepting the foreign aircraft, while an hour later Marshal Siergiey Biryuzov arrived there to supervise related actions. Meanwhile Khrushchev learned of the incident and as could have been expected was indignant, suspecting that a US reconnaissance mission on 1 May was a deliberate provocation. He ordered the intruder to be destroyed at all cost and was voicing his displeasure with the V-PVO's inability to deal with it. In response Marshal Biryuzov exclaimed that if he could, he would turn himself into a missile and down the 'damned intruder'.[2]

Meanwhile, air defences all over the southern USSR were placed on full combat alert and at the same time all civilian aircraft were

A Su-9 in the process of taking-off: notable are four empty launch rails for RS-2U air-to-air missiles, probably the same or similar configuration as the example piloted by Captain Igor Mientiukov on 1 May 1960. (Tom Cooper Collection)

instructed to land at the nearest airfield. With the skies cleared the Soviets were now contemplating how to deal with the intruder. The longer its flight went on, the better it was tracked by multiple radars, and eventually it became obvious that it was heading for Sverdlovsk. This was good news for the Soviets because the city was defended by SAM sites and fighter units were also based in the vicinity. For these reasons there was a realistic chance of finally bringing down the American reconnaissance aircraft.

Kamikaze – Soviet Style

Since nobody could guarantee that the U-2 would enter the engagement zone of the SAMs it was decided to scramble interceptors of the V-PVO first. Bearing in mind Khrushchev's directive 'to destroy the target at all cost', General Yevgeny Savitskiy – commander of the Fighter Aviation of the V-PVO – issued an order to engage the intruder with all flights on alert located in the area of the foreign aircraft's course, and to ram it if necessary.

The dubious privilege of carrying out this order fell to Captain Igor Mientiukov. It so

A nice study of an entire row of V-PVO Su-9s, together with five pilots wearing the VKK-3 high-altitude pressure suits (for details, see colour section). (Tom Cooper Collection)

happened that – by pure coincidence – on 30 April 1960 he made a refuelling stop at Kolcovo air base outside Sverdlovsk, while delivering a brand-new Su-9 from the manufacturer to an operational unit. Instead of continuing his voyage on the next day, he was ordered to scramble and destroy a high-flying target. Because his Sukhoi was in ferry configuration, it carried no armament: his jet was designed without any guns, and had no air-to-air missiles installed because none were available at Kolcovo. Seemingly, Mientiukov's task was impossible to fulfil, but the order was an order and he scrambled in great haste. Once airborne, the pilot established radio contact with ground control, and not only received information about the target but also a clear order to ram it. The mission was for all practical purpose suicidal, for even if the pilot survived the collision the effects of a high-altitude ejection under such circumstances were likely to be lethal.

Captain Mientiukov was guided by ground control to intercept the U-2 on a rear chase course. When the distance to the target was about 25km the pilot was ordered to jettison external fuel tanks and to ignite the afterburner. The speed of his mount rapidly rose to Mach 1.9-2.0, while he climbed to 20,000m. Just as the distance to the U-2 decreased to 12 km the American aircraft made a turn and the Soviet pilot – who still had no visual contact with the target – was instructed to follow. However, when flying at such a high speed and altitude, the Su-9 – like most of other interceptors of the time – was not particularly

manoeuvrable. As a result, Captain Mientiukov overshot the target by 8,000 metres. Considering his high speed, this was actually not as much as it might appear at first glance. However, he was now in front of his target and out of position to 'simply' turn and re-attack. Therefore, ground control ordered Mientiukov to cut the afterburner and lose speed. However, just as the Sukhoi-pilot complied with the order, he received the next one: to disengage and leave the area, immediately: in the meantime, Power's U-2 was about to enter the engagement zone of the SAMs protecting Sverdlovsk, and the first missile salvo was already airborne. Now it was better for friendly aircraft to get out of the way.

Success – at last

The first to open fire was one of four missile battalions responsible for the defence of Sverdlovsk and assigned to the 4th Independent Army of the V-PVO: the unit under the command of Captain Nikolai Sheludko. The U-2 literally skimmed its engagement zone, but nevertheless Sheludko ordered a missile salvo to be launched. Unsurprisingly, the 'spy aircraft' was already out of range by the time the missiles reached its altitude, resulting in their self-destruction. Meanwhile the U-2 entered the engagement zone of the next S-75 SAM-site, commanded by Major Mikhail Voronov. At 08:36 this unit fired its first surface-to-air missile.[3] Initially, only one of the brand-new V-750VN (13D) missiles with improved range and maximum engagement altitude was launched, because a safety lock prevented

A V-750VN/13D missile in the process of lifting off from its SM-90 launcher. The fact that Sverdlovsk was protected by one brigade of the V-PVO, consisting of four battalions (or SAM-sites) equipped with these brand-new missiles proved decisive for the Soviet success on 1 May 1960. (Albert Grandolini Collection)

the launching of the usual salvo. Nevertheless, more missiles followed shortly after. Immediately afterwards, Voronov's operators reported that the target on their screen began to 'blink': this either meant it was hit and disintegrating – or employing electronic countermeasures. In fact, the first missile had detonated behind Powers' U-2, and its blast and fragments had already caused crippling damage. As a result, the US aircraft was falling from the sky and breaking apart in the process. Locked inside their command post, Voronov and his subordinates could not see the drama developing above them, as Powers struggled to get out of his cockpit: all they had was the 'radar picture' on the screens in front of them – which was open to interpretation. Indeed, because they could not take it for granted that the U-2 had actually been shot down, Voronov ordered additional missiles to be launched, and initially did not report the destruction of the target.

Nothing but Trouble

Actually, Powers had already experienced problems before his U-2 was engaged by Soviet SAMs. As first, he had to disengage his faulty autopilot. Because he was already deep within Soviet airspace, he decided to continue the mission in manual mode. By the time he approached Sverdlovsk, he had been airborne for four hours and, while nearing the city, made a turn to photograph installations to the south-west of it. Apparently, this was the manoeuvre that spoiled Mientiukov's ramming attack, thus saving the life of the courageous Soviet interceptor pilot. In turn, from the point of view of the US pilot, there was no indication of the impending disaster. On the contrary, the first sign for Powers that he was facing major problems was a dull explosion, causing his aircraft to lurch forward, and followed by a bright orange glow that lit the skies for several seconds. Meanwhile underway at almost 70,500ft (21,488m) Powers attempted to regain control of his mount, but to no avail. The right wing then broke off, followed by the left one, and the aircraft flipped out of control,

ending in a spin, falling tail-down, probably because of the engine's weight. For the pilot, there was no way out but to save himself – not an easy task, because in order to eject Powers had to move the seat back and get his legs from underneath the instrument panel. Due to

Senior Lieutenant Sergey Ivanovich Safronov, the V-PVO MiG-19 pilot and a U-2 hunter, shot down and killed by V-PVO S-75s on 1 May 1960. (TASS)

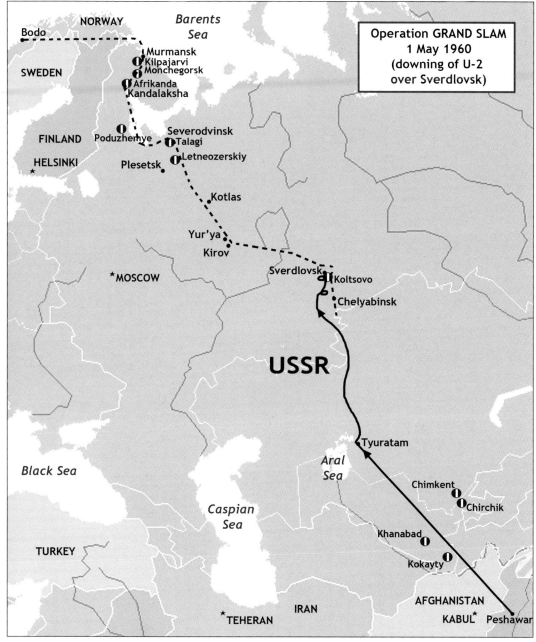

A map showing the route taken by Powers during Operation Grand Slam, based on Soviet radar tracks. Notably, after losing his autopilot, the CIA flier experienced significant problems with keeping a steady course. Also notable is that, according to Soviet data, Powers did two full 360-degree turns – one south and one west of Sverdlovsk. The dotted line indicates the course Powers was supposed to fly after passing Sverdlovsk – part of which was to bring him directly over an entire chain of major Soviet air bases on the Kola Peninsula. (Map by Tom Cooper)

for most of the involved Soviets was that it still had to be shot down. By now, two MiG-19s were airborne and approaching the engagement zone: the aircraft were flown by Captain Boris Aivazian and Senior Lieutenant Sergey Safronov. Earlier experiences had clearly demonstrated that the MiGs were unable to catch a U-2. One could always hope for a lucky opportunity: if nothing else, the US aircraft could have lost some altitude due to a malfunction or other reason.

Once airborne, Aivazian and Safronov were guided by ground control: both pilots then sighted debris falling from the sky and reported this. These were the remains of the downed U-2. Unfortunately, nobody on the ground realised this at this point in time. Therefore, when 'unidentified aircraft' entered the engagement zone of the next SAM-battalion, its commander – Major Shugayev – ordered his subordinates to open fire. Once again, the V-750s proved their deadly effectiveness. Tragically, this time against a friendly aircraft.

All of a sudden, an explosion enveloped the MiG-19 flown by Senior Lieutenant Safronov. The pilot ejected but was mortally wounded and probably died under the parachute before reaching the ground. His lifeless body was found by locals near the village Degtyarka, west of Sverdlovsk. Captain Aivazian had more luck: he promptly dove, thus avoiding further missiles streaking in his direction.

A subsequent analysis revealed that – other than Major Voronov's hesitations – the main reason for this incident was poor coordination between various air defence assets. Moreover, the Soviets concluded that the IFF-transponders on their MiGs either did not work or were transmitting the wrong code. Because of this, the interceptors showed on the radar screens of Major Shugayev's unit as 'unidentified', instead of 'friendly'. This finding was contested by Captain Aivazian, who stated that an IFF check was performed before take-off. In an attempt to reconcile these contradictory claims it was also reported that the IFF codes of the fighters were not changed as they should have been from the ones used in April to those valid in May. Regardless of how the problem came about and who was to blame, one thing stood clear: the dramatic demise of the MiG was a spectacular and embarrassing case of fratricide. For this reason, Senior Lieutenant Safronov's death was kept secret for many years.

the spin-inducted g-forces, the seat jammed and would not move. Hence, Powers could not eject but had to bail out manually instead. He jettisoned the canopy, unfastened his seat harness and – after hanging on his oxygen-supply pipe for a while – found himself clear of the cockpit. Had he ejected with his seat, a self-destruct mechanism (including 2.5-3lbs. i.e. 1.13–1.36 kg of cyclonite) would have been activated automatically: however, because the American pilot bailed out, this had to be activated manually. Powers failed to do that because he could not reach the switch after being sucked out of the cockpit.[4] As a result the U-2's wreckage, with cameras and film, came down relatively intact.

An Unnecessary Death

Because there was no report citing the destruction of the foreign aircraft (Voronov and his crew were not aware of being successful for some 30 minutes afterwards), the seemingly logical conclusion

Wreckage of Powers' U-2, together with a group of local Soviet civilians. (TASS, via Albert Grandolini)

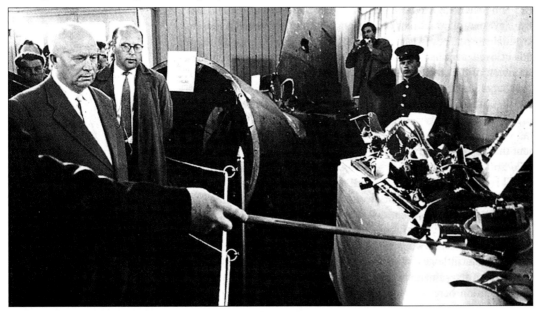

Soviet leader Nikita Khrushchev in the process of being shown the wreckage and equipment of Power's U-2. The success of the V-PVO was ably exploited by Moscow as a major propaganda coup. (TASS, via Albert Grandolini)

The Aftermath

Altogether the PVO SAM units involved had fired no fewer than 15 V-750 missiles on 1 May. When Major Voronov finally concluded that the foreign aircraft was shot down, he reported the target's destruction and ordered one of the battalion's officers, Captain Kazantsev, to organize an armed search party in order to apprehend its pilot. It soon turned out that the latter measure was not necessary.

Once out of the cockpit Powers was briefly held up by his oxygen hose, but it soon broke loose and he fell freely earthwards. The American pilot's parachute automatically opened at a predetermined altitude and Powers safely floated down to earth. Since he was literally in the middle of the Soviet Union hiding or offering resistance was futile. Powers did not make use of a poisoned needle that he had been provided with (there was no obligation to do so and it would have been inhuman and unenforceable anyway) and allowed approaching locals to take him into a car and drive to a kolkhoz (a state-owned farm). There, he was kept in the office until the authorities arrived and picked him up. Subsequently Powers was first taken to Sverdlovsk, then brought to the local airfield and finally taken aboard an aircraft destined for Moscow. According to some accounts he was briefly shown to the

Powers as seen after his capture, still wearing the MC-3 high-pressure suit (see colour section for details). (TASS, via Albert Grandolini)

Soviet pilots who had attempted to intercept him (they had meanwhile landed) in order to give them a symbolic reward for their efforts.

As soon as the downing of the intruder had been positively confirmed the news was reported to Khrushchev. A special commission was swiftly dispatched from the Soviet capital and arrived at the scene within hours. Its task was to investigate the events which took place as well as to gather material evidence, especially the remains of the American aircraft. The U-2 broke up in the air with not only the wings but also the tail and other parts separating from the aircraft's main body as it was going down. Yet despite being scattered on the ground over an area of several square kilometres, the wreckage of the U-2 was quickly located and collected. Among the items recovered, of particular interest to the Soviets was the photographic equipment and the rolls of film it contained.

After being examined by Soviet experts the remains of the U-2 were put on display in Moscow's Gorky Park and were shown to the Soviet leadership, journalists and the general public. [5]

Last but not least, it is worth noting that Major Mikhail Voronov – the first successful U-2-hunter ever – was decorated with the Order of the Red Banner, receiving medal no. 530334. The principal reason for which he was not put forward for the Hero of the Soviet Union title and medal was that the shooting down of Powers' U-2 also led to the fratricidal downing of Safronov's MiG-19. In the formal announcement citing 21 servicemen who were decorated for their deeds in connection with the shooting down of the American aircraft, Safronov was listed without the word "posthumously" being added next to his name.[6]

6

AFTER EFFECTS OF POWERS' DOWNING

Once the Americans realized that the U-2 had disappeared – presumably being lost – the National Aeronautics and Space Administration issued a press release claiming that one of its aircraft performing a high-altitude research mission had gone missing. Further it was claimed that the pilot radioed a message about supposed oxygen problems. It was implied that the pilot had fallen unconscious, but with the autopilot engaged the aircraft flew on penetrating into Soviet territory. The cover story was agreed on beforehand but had not been honed concerning its finer points and thus lacked credibility; no one really expected the U-2 to come down in the middle of the Soviet Union. Last but not least, Powers had not been briefed on what the cover story would be either.[1]

Having intentionally waited for the US announcement before making his own, Khrushchev had the information released that a reconnaissance aircraft had been shot down over Soviet territory, but he did not yet reveal that the pilot of the said aircraft had been captured alive. The Americans maintained their cover story only to be exposed with Khrushchev's announcement on 7 May 1960 that the U-2's pilot was alive and in Soviet custody. At that point the United States was put into a decidedly unfavourable position both politically as well as propaganda wise. Moreover, President Eisenhower personally found himself in a situation demanding that he either took responsibility for this act and its results or appeared not to be in control of the government and its agencies. Being the man who led the Allied forces to victory in mankind's greatest war Eisenhower was not short of personal courage and took responsibility for what had happened. He also argued, not without having a point, that Soviet secretiveness necessitated vigilance and thus overflights of the Soviet Union were,

in essence, not signs of aggressive intent but defensive cautiousness.

The planned summit in Paris collapsed because Khrushchev demanded an apology from Eisenhower – a demand to which the latter would not yield. This halted efforts to bring about better relations between the United States and the Soviet Union, a not insignificant matter considering that both were nuclear armed, though at that time the US held the advantage in this regard. Considering the way the Soviets handled the aftermath of the U-2's downing and the capture of its pilot they arguably extracted the maximum short term propaganda effect from the event and caused the United States, as well as the country's president, much embarrassment. Having said that they failed to secure any significant long-term advantage which they might have attained had they been somewhat more conciliatory. It is an old wisdom that being gracious while having the upper hand is not a sign of weakness and more frequently than not pays off.

Powers' Fate

Having been flown from Sverdlovsk to Moscow, Powers was brought to and then held in the Lubyanka, the notorious headquarters of the State Security Committee (Komitet Gosudarstvennoy Bezopasnosti, KGB), in Moscow. While not tortured or abused, he was denied sleep and repeatedly interrogated. Ironically, the CIA failed to properly train its pilots for such an eventuality, and the downed flier had to improvise: he tried his best to only provide information available in open sources or deducible from the examination of his aircraft. Once the interrogation was over Powers was charged with espionage against the USSR and put on trial. The trial was publicised to the maximum. Although this was not a classic Soviet show trial, the charges were

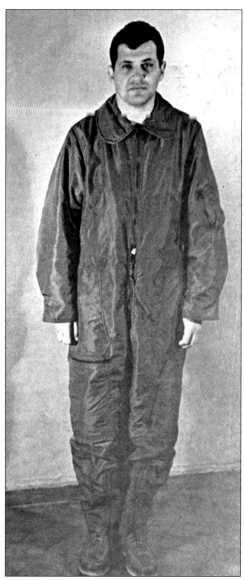

Francis Gary Powers in Soviet captivity. Ironically, he attracted far more public attention than the man who commanded the SAM-site that shot him down, Major Mikhail Voronov. (TASS, via Albert Grandolini)

as a test-pilot for the Lockheed Corporation, but lost this job after co-authoring the book *Operation Overflight*. Eventually, he worked as a pilot for a TV station in Los Angeles and was killed in a helicopter crash on 1 August 1977. Francis Gary Powers was laid to rest with honours at Arlington National Cemetery. The Distinguished Flying Cross was awarded to him only posthumously.

In comparison, most of the V-PVO officers involved in his shoot-down were highly decorated and continued serving for years longer.

A Hot Period of the Cold War

The downing of the U-2 brought such high-altitude flights over the Soviet Union to a halt once and for all. However, intelligence-gathering missions of a peripheral nature continued. Such were performed by, amongst others, Boeing RB-47H reconnaissance bombers of the USAF's 38th Strategic Reconnaissance Squadron (SRS), based at Forbes Air Force Base (AFB) in Kansas, and from RAF Brize Norton in Great Britain. For example, on 1 July 1960, exactly two months after Powers' U-2 was shot down, the RB-47H (FY serial number 53-4281) launched from the latter base for another overflight. The aircraft was crewed by Major Willard Palm (mission commander), Captain Freeman B Olmstead (pilot), and Captain John McKone (navigator), and three specialists operating electronic equipment, so-called 'crows': Major Eugene Posa, Captain Dean Philips, and Captain Oscar Goforth. The latter three were all packed into the cramped compartment with their electronic gear installed inside the bomb bay.[2]

At that point of time, the USA – more precisely: Strategic Air Command (SAC) – enjoyed an undisputable advantage in regards of nuclear-capable strategic bombers vis-à-vis the USSR. Washington could have hoped to successfully wage and win a nuclear war against Moscow, especially as the SAC-operated bombers were capable of launching from the continental USA over the Arctic to attack the full width of the Soviet Union from the northern direction. To accomplish such a mission, air defences along the northern coast of the USSR had to be either destroyed or avoided. Moreover, the bomber-crews involved had to be provided with detailed radar maps of their potential targets. For these reasons SAC regularly tasked its RB-47 crews with flying electronic- and radar-reconnaissance of the high north of the Soviet Union.

The mission of the RB-47H piloted by Olmstead was underway for several hours when the bomber was intercepted by at least one Soviet jet: a MiG-19 of the 174th Guards Fighter Aviation Regiment (*gvardeyskiy istrebitel'nyy aviatsionnyy polk*, GIAP), flown by Captain Vasyli Polyakov.

Tragedies and Ironies

Accounts differ not only on how the situation developed but even where it took place. The Soviets maintained that their MiGs caught the RB-47H well within their airspace, right off Cape Svyatoy Nos, whereas the Americans claimed that the jet was never closer than 30 miles (about 55 kilometres) to that location. Polyakov would have first taken station off the bomber's right wing and rocked his own wings in a clear signal for the intercepted Americans to follow his instructions. Because the crew of the SAC jet failed to comply, the Soviet pilot then distanced, before returning to make two strafing passes in the course of which he fired 111 rounds from his 30mm cannon. Acting as gunner, Captain McKone deployed his aircraft's tail turret mounting two 20mm cannon to return fire, but either the radar directing these, or the guns themselves jammed. The result was unavoidable: Polyakov's shells caused crippling damage and the RB-47H went down. The flight crew ejected: Captains McKone and Olmsted were rescued by a Soviet fishing trawler; Major Palm's body was found a day later. Tragically,

spurious: even if knowingly violating the Soviet airspace, the defendant was effectively prevented from committing the crime for which he was charged. Because it was pointless to deny his intelligence-gathering activity he 'confessed', pleaded guilty and made a statement to the effect of being sorry for his acts. Found guilty, on 19 August 1960 Francis Gary Powers was sentenced to ten years of prison. From the point of view of the Soviet authorities, this had the desired effect.

Fortunately, the downed airman did not serve his full sentence: on 10 February 1962, he was exchanged in the course of the famous 'spy swap', staged at the Glienicke Bridge in Berlin, for the Soviet spy Rudolf Abel (a.k.a. William August Fisher), and two US students (William Pryor and Marvin Makinen) who were arrested for, literally, 'being at the wrong place, at the wrong point in time'. Although quickly returned to the USA, Powers found himself exposed to entirely unfair public critique, foremost by the proponents of the idea that he should have not allowed himself to be captured alive. He was extensively debriefed by the CIA, representatives of the Lockheed Corporation, and the USAF, and then underwent a hearing at the Armed Services Select Committee of the US Senate. Eventually exonerated of any wrongdoing, and praised for his actions and conduct, he was decorated with the Intelligence Star medal in 1965 but was not permitted to continue serving with the US Air Force. Instead, he found employment

A Boeing RB-47H of the 55th SRW, nicely showing multiple antennae and receivers. The three 'crows' were packed inside a modified bomb-bay, visible as a dark-grey 'bulb' at the lower portion of the fuselage, directly below the wing – and behind the big 'teardrop-shaped' antenna. (USAF)

A row of Soviet MiG-19 interceptors at an air base on the Kola Peninsula. (TASS, via Albert Grandolini)

the three crows never stood chance: all perished while still inside the cramped cabin. Only the body of Major Posa was found later, but – for unknown reasons – never returned to the USA.

The post-scriptum of this incident is loaded with irony. While nearly all of the contemporary Western intelligence reports assessed the average Soviet fighter-pilot as a de-facto poorly-trained 'bus driver', expected only to know how to take-off and land, and otherwise limited in his decision-making to follow orders from ground control – which was supposed to tell him not only when to jettison drop tanks, but also when to activate his radar and open fire – it was only decades later that it turned out that Captain Polyakov acted entirely on his own initiative. Foremost, at no time during his interception of the RB-47H on 1 July 1960 was he ordered to apply lethal force. Instead, he invoked the standing order to destroy any aircraft violating Soviet airspace. Indeed, Polyakov's superiors were startled at the fact that he opened fire, and initially suspected him of having opened fire at one of

the Soviet Naval Aviation's Tupolev Tu-16 bombers. It was only after a thorough investigation that they realised what exactly had happened – and that, indeed, a very serious international incident had occurred. Because it turned out that Khrushchev personally was highly satisfied with the outcome, the entire affair was treated in the vein of, 'teaching the Americans a lesson'. Therefore, Polyakov not only avoided being court-martialled, but was decorated with the Order of the Red Banner medal.

To bolster the irony, some Soviet – and subsequently Russian – historians did not find this enough. They stressed that Polyakov's resolve to shoot down the reconnaissance aircraft would have been 'strengthened' by the fact that the RB-47H was heading for a secret Soviet Navy submarine base. Arguably, the latter appears rather unlikely: not only were all of the Soviet Navy's submarine bases 'off limits' to anybody else but authorised personnel, and generally unknown even to members of other branches of the armed forces;

but, if a Captain of the V-PVO had any knowledge about that kind of a facility, this was certainly no 'secret'.

The situation was not much better on the Western side of the tribune, either. The two surviving members of the RB-47H's crew were brought to the Lubyanka: for a while, Moscow contemplated putting them on trial for espionage, but eventually decided not to. Instead, both were released on 24 January 1961 as a good-will gesture to the newly-inaugurated US President John F. Kennedy. Contrary to Powers, later on, they received a heroes' welcome – including a reception by Kennedy at the White House.[3]

Eventually, this series of major incidents from the spring of 1960 marked the start of probably the hottest period of the Cold War. However, anybody expecting them to mark its culmination was soon to be proven wrong.

7
CARIBBEAN CONFRONTATION

While the shoot-down of the U-2 flown by Francis Garry Powers over the USSR is a well-known, widely publicised affair, a similar incident over Cuba is nowadays often forgotten. There are a number of reasons for this: among others is the fact that the loss of one man and a single aircraft during such a massive affair as the Cuban Missile Crisis of October 1962 is likely to appear as trivial, especially in comparison to the prospect of a world-wide nuclear Armageddon. However, the incident could have escalated the situation at a crucial point in time – precisely when Moscow and Washington were neck-deep into deescalating it. Meanwhile, many of the restrictions upon the related reporting – imposed by both superpowers during the Cold War – have been lifted, and nowadays it is possible to provide an almost complete reconstruction of the 'Hunt for the U-2' over Cuba.

Overture

For many years, the Caribbean island of Cuba was under the dictatorial rule of Fulgencio Batista, his family and friends. His heavy-handed oppression proved highly unpopular but failed to quell dissent and provoked an armed rebellion. The latter proved impossible to defeat by military means, and on 1 January 1959 Batista fled the country, leaving it to the victorious rebels led by Fidel Castro. Instead of ending Cuba's woes, this merely opened a new chapter in its difficult history.

A CIA map showing 'Reconnaissance Objectives in Cuba': all the facilities in question became the object of special interest for all available reconnaissance platforms of the US armed forces and intelligence agencies in October 1962. (NSA)

Initially after seizing power, Castro went to great extents to – at least verbally – distance himself from communist and socialist ideologies for which he was trounced in the USA. Moreover, he attempted to maintain at least minimum proper relations with the USA. However, not only did Washington ignore him: private interests found themselves badly hurt by his decision to nationalise vast US possessions on the island. Indeed, the changes the post-revolutionary government brought about both in the social sphere and in regards of the economy – foremost the ownership of assets – severely infringed too many US interests. Cuba thus soon found itself exposed to a US embargo, followed by a severe deterioration of political and diplomatic relations. On 3 January 1961, Washington closed its embassy in Havana.

Apparently at least, the days of Castro's rule over Cuba were now numbered, and the USA had already begun planning an armed invasion of the island by a proxy force before withdrawing its diplomatic representatives. Reconnaissance was an indispensable part of the related preparations, and – even more so because the operation in question was run by the CIA – the U-2s were called upon to do their task. Undertaken on 26 and 27 October 1960, the first two overflights were run by the agency from Laughlin AFB in Texas. However, because of the cloud cover, both failed to meet their expectations. Langley thus requested permission for additional missions, and Washington approved three overflights. Undertaken on 27 November, 5 and 11 December 1960, these produced at least 'satisfactory' results. Unsurprisingly considering Cuba had no means to hunt the CIA's U-2s, additional operations followed in the next year. The first two were flown on 19 and 21 March, but they were just a prelude: 15 further overflights were undertaken starting from 6 April 1961 in order to provide photographic coverage of the failed Bay of Pigs invasion, which took place between 17 and 20 April of the same year.[1]

Enter the Big Brother

The failure of the Bay of Pigs invasion brought no respite in tensions between Cuba and the USA. On the contrary, the worst was yet to follow, and it was soon the involvement of the USSR on the side of Castro's government that was to dominate this affair.

Contrary to accusations widely published in the USA of the 1950s and 1960s, originally at least, Moscow was entirely disinterested in the island, and – at most – expressed only lukewarm support for the Cuban revolutionaries. To the Soviets, the entire affair appeared to be one of the 'typical revolutions, taking place at regular intervals all over the Latin America and the Caribbean' of the time – and thus contained 'no revolutionary aspects', at least no more than a group of armed men attempting to overthrow a local dictator, before taking over to become dictators in their own right. Moreover, Latin America was considered a 'firmly US sphere of influence' and was – geographically – much too far away for the Soviets to even consider establishing links. However, when Cuba faced arms and economic embargoes from the USA, and could no longer sell sugar, its primary product, to the US, its principal export market, and especially once its new ruler publicly declared himself a Marxist-Leninist, the Soviets stepped in with a trade agreement the essence of which was an exchange of sugar for fuel, oil and lubricants. Thus, the Soviets not only became involved, but even considered the situation beneficial for them: they were now in control of a position virtually on 'America's doorstep'.

The latter was a fact that was, as of 1962, of immense strategic importance. At the time, the USSR was at a distinct disadvantage vis-à-vis the USA in regards of the means of deploying nuclear weapons. Not only had the development of the much-hyped R-7 intercontinental ballistic missile reached a dead-end – and that it would take the Soviets nearly a decade to bridge the gap to similar weapons systems under development in the USA – in 1961 US ballistic missiles with nuclear warheads were deployed in Italy and Turkey, from where they could reach Moscow in a matter of 10 minutes. In contrast, the Soviets had no nuclear forces in the relative proximity of the USA, and even their largest strategic bombers – of which, as mentioned above, there were

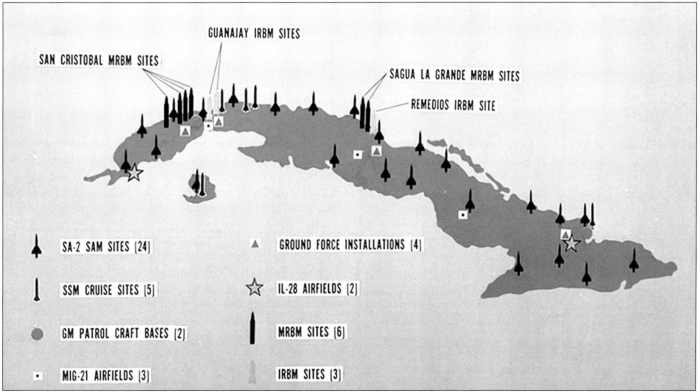

Another CIA map, this time one denoting the type of Soviet bases on Cuba as of October 1962. (NSA)

few – lacked the range to reach their targets in the USA and return to their bases. Moreover, no improvement for these issues was in sight. All of this suddenly changed when the government in Havana began gravitating towards Moscow.

Of course, there were other reasons of military and political nature for the Soviets to become involved on the island – and these were often closely interlinked. Cuba was not only ideally positioned for the deployment of intermediate-range ballistic missiles equipped with nuclear warheads, but its government also proved eager to host such weapons because it feared another possible US invasion attempt. In May 1962, Castro and Khrushchev thus agreed to deploy and station Soviet nuclear-armed missiles in Cuba, including both intermediate range ballistic missiles and tactical cruise missiles – both of which, obviously, achieved strategic importance as a result.

Operation Anadyr

The deployment of Soviet forces to Cuba was run within the framework of Operation Anadyr. The first to be deployed were substantial aviation and air defence elements. These included the Volgograd-based 11th Missile Air Defence Division equipped with S-75 SAM systems (which included the 507th Air Defence Regiment), and the Kubinka AB-based 32rd GIAP equipped with MiG-21F-13 interceptors.[2] Pilots of the later unit were considered the Soviet aviation's cream of the crop, and the entire wing was no stranger to expeditionary deployment overseas: on the contrary, it was fresh from a recent deployment to Indonesia, where it helped work-up the local MiG-21-equipped squadron. The 11th Missile Air Defence Division was selected because it achieved above-average results in training, and a large part of its personnel were members of the Communist Party of the USSR or the Komsomol. With the exception of some officers that travelled by transport aircraft, most of the aircraft and personnel reached Cuba by ship: for example, the 32nd GIAP – re-designated as the 213rd IAP for its deployment abroad – embarked the merchants *Volgoles* and *Nikolayevsk*, while the 11th Missile Air Defence Division travelled on board the merchant *Latvia*.[3]

Of course, all the related movements were kept strictly secret, and it was only once the all the ships in question reached the Atlantic Ocean that their skippers opened a sealed envelope instructing them to inform everybody on board – senior officers first – about their destination. Certainly enough, Moscow went to great extents to maintain secrecy, but all in vain: thanks to repeated overflights by U-2s during the spring and summer of 1962, the CIA was kept well-informed about the Soviet build-up. Moreover, the overflights continued into October, with the only change being that on the 12th of the month, President Kennedy ordered all the related operational decisions to be taken by the US Air Force. The first USAF U-2 overflight of Cuba had already returned with rather startling results. On 14 October 1962, Major Richard S Heyser brought back photographs showing clear evidence of the Soviets deploying ballistic missiles capable of delivering nuclear warheads. With such a threat literally on 'America's doorstep'; Kennedy promptly provided blanket approval for as many U-2 missions as required to provide a full coverage of the island.

Therefore, during the following week, the U-2s conducted multiple missions each day – and their operations were supplanted by low-altitude operations undertaken by Vought RF-8 Crusaders of VFP-62 of the US Navy, and US Air Force McDonnell RF-101 Voodoos.[4]

Cold War Encounters

Once on Cuba, the 213th IAP was home-based at Santa Clara AB, while the 11th Missile Air Defence Division established its HQ in Camaguey. Of course, in order to cover as much of the local airspace

Underside view of an unarmed MiG-21F-13 as seen on landing. Aircraft of the 32nd GIAP (re-designated as the 213th IAP) deployed on Cuba in 1962 wore Cuban national insignia, but retained their typical, large, two-digit, 'bort' numbers on the nose (for details, see colour section). (TASS, via Albert Grandolini)

as possible, the latter had to distribute its elements quite widely. Therefore, S-75 SAM-sites were constructed at about 60-80 kilometres (37-50 miles) from each other. Even then, and although their crews were quick in preparing their equipment, all the air defence units were ordered to stand down, at least for the time being. On the contrary, MiG-pilots were airborne from 18 September 1962, and flew intensively from then on. Indeed, because of the intensive activity of US reconnaissance aircraft, direct encounters between the 'Cold War Warriors' soon became unavoidable.[5]

The first direct encounter took place a few days later, when a flight of MiGs led by Lieutenant-Colonel Sergey Perovsky (Deputy Commander of the 213th IAP) came across two aircraft which he (mis)identified as RF-101s. Despite the fact that the Soviets were actually in the process of re-locating from Santa Clara to San Antonio AB, their aircraft carried live R-3S air-to-air missiles. Upon sighting the American aircraft, Lieutenant-Colonel Perovsky requested ground control for permission to engage them – only to be categorically forbidden to do so. Another incident took place on 4 November 1962. This time a MiG with Major Dmitry Bobrov at the controls was returning from a training mission when he was ordered by ground control to intercept and chase away two aircraft misidentified as RF-101s. The latter were actually two Lockheed F-104 Starfighter interceptors from the 479th Tactical Fighter Wing (TFW) of the USAF. Although his aircraft was 'armed' only with two captive training missiles, and his gun was not loaded, the Soviet pilot manoeuvred to gain an advantageous position, but once the Americans realised that they had unwelcomed company both turned in the direction of Florida and distanced from Cuban airspace at high speed – probably doing the most prudent thing under the circumstances.

The third encounter with US aircraft involved Major Shtoda, and the circumstances were similar to previous ones: the Soviet pilot was

In 1957, following successful high-altitude overflights of Eastern Europe by Canberra reconnaissance bombers of the Royal Air Force, the CIA furnished several RB-57As – essentially the first US-manufactured variant of the British-designed Canberra – to the 4th Squadron, 6th Group, 5th Wing, ROCAF. Like all RB-57As of the USAF, all were painted in glossy black overall, and wore their serials and ROCAF registrations applied in red. After undertaking dozens of high-risk missions, the jet illustrated here (52-1431/5642) was intercepted by a pair of PLAAF interceptors (probably MiG-17F) over Shandong, and shot down, on 18 February 1958. The pilot, Guang-Huia Chao, was killed. (Artwork by Tom Cooper)

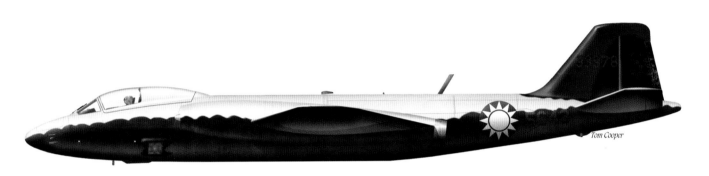

With the loss of one RB-57A proving that further operations of that variant over mainland China would be suicidal, the CIA furnished three more advanced RB-57Ds to the 4th Squadron ROCAF. All were left in the livery already applied in the USA, consisting of matt white on top surfaces, and matt black on sides and undersurfaces. Like the RB-57As before them, they also received large Taiwanese national insignia on the rear fuselage and the top surface of the left wing, and their serials and the ROCAF registration in red. 4th Squadron's RB-57Ds flew 15 successful missions over the PRC until the jet shown here (53-3978/5643) was shot down by S-75s of the 2nd Surface-to-Air Guided Missile Battalion, PLA, becoming the first ever to be shot down by SAMs. The pilot, Ying Chin Wong, was killed. (Artwork by Tom Cooper)

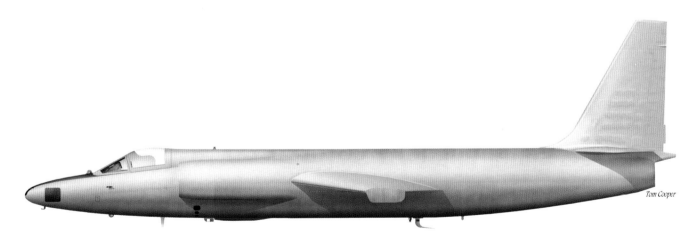

The original J-57-powered U-2As operated by the CIA went into action in 1956 painted in highly-polished clear lacquer only, and wearing not even the typical stencilling related to their ejection seats. The only other colours applied included a small anti-glare panel in front of the cockpit and the dielectric antenna on either side of the nose, both in black. The sun shade was always applied in white colour, on the inside of the cockpit. In an attempt to make them less conspicuous, in 1958 the CIA began testing various camouflage colours, including at least one reportedly decreasing the radar echo of the jet. Compared to later variants, the U-2As wore relatively few antennae and other gear: their primary mission-equipment consisted of either Type A or Type B camera set installed in the Q-bay, directly behind the cockpit. (Artwork by Tom Cooper)

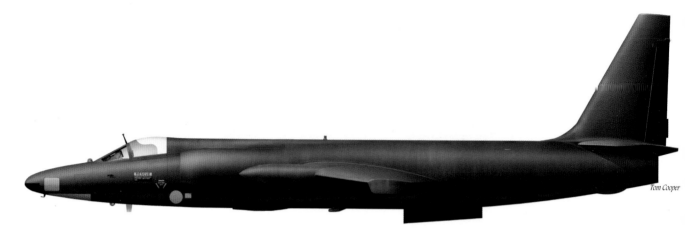

By the time the U-2s returned to the skies over the USSR in late 1959 much of the fleet had been upgraded to the J-75-powered U-2C standard. Moreover, many were painted in the semi-gloss version of the USN's Sea Blue – originally designated AN607 non-specular sea blue, later FS25042 – and, later on, in its matt version (FS35042). This was valid for 'Article 360', the aircraft flown by Francis G Powers on 1 May 1960. The jet was configured for its fateful mission as shown here, including the SIGINT System 6 (identifiable by antennae on either side of the nose and the front portion of the Q-bay), B-camera installation with seven windows (in the Q-bay), Giant Stride slipper tanks, and the ventral fin including antennae for the SIGINT Systems 3 and 6. Finally, it carried no 'canoe' dorsal fairing during its final mission, and no tail number. (Artwork by Tom Cooper)

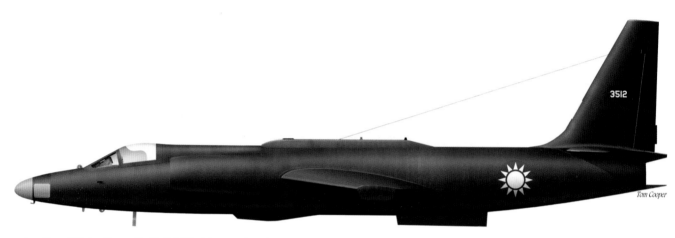

A reconstruction of Major Chang Li-yi's U-2C 'Article 358', shot down over the PRC on 10 January 1965. Painted in non-specular sea blue overall (FS 35042), this aircraft may have had 'coke bottle' intakes. The exact configuration of the equipment installed in the Q-bay and its underbelly antennae remains unclear: this artwork shows what can be reconstructed from the available photographs and various artworks. At least as uncertain is the application of national markings and the installation of the 'canoe' dorsal fairing. Available photographs of the wreckage taken immediately after the shoot-down show the large national insignia on the rear fuselage. Recent photographs of its wreckage on display in the PRC show a large national insignia on the forward fuselage: most likely, these were pieces of several different aircraft used to 'complete' the wreckage of the ROCAF's 3512. (Artwork by Tom Cooper)

The USAF-operated U-2s initially wore the original bare metal overall livery until 1962, when gloss light grey was applied on some to help protect them from corrosion, while others received the same AN607 non-specular sea blue as most of the CIA-operated fleet. The latter was the case with the U-2A flown by Major Rudolf Anderson over Cuba on 27 October 1962. Contrary to the CIA-operated examples, this aircraft received the full national insignia, a big service title, and the 'last five' of its FY-serial number (56-6676) on the fin. The jet should have also received the later, deeper but shorter version of the Sugar Scoop: a plate attached to the lower portion of the exhaust, designed to better protect it from infra-red homing missiles – like the R-3S carried by the MiG-21s. (Artwork by Tom Cooper)

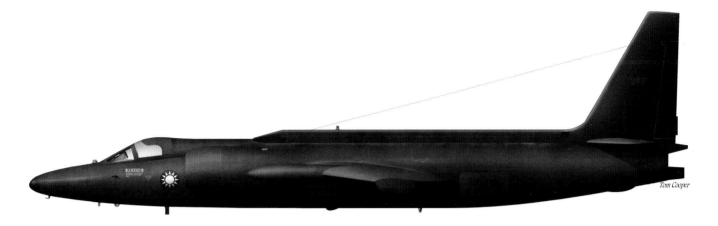

By 1965, USAF-operated U-2s were repainted in a matt black colour known as 'black velvet', which – reportedly – helped reduce their radar-echo. Correspondingly, U-2C/F/Gs still operated by the 35th Black Cat Squadron, ROCAF, received the same livery. Three years later, their 'interim' intakes (bulged only in the horizontal, but not in the vertical axis) were replaced by significantly bigger 'Coke bottle' intakes, meanwhile developed for the much-improved U-2R. By 1967, they were equipped with additional underwing drop tanks, further stretching their already impressive endurance. As far as is known, these jets wore their national markings on the forward fuselage, below the cockpit, and had three-digit tail numbers applied in red. (Artwork by Tom Cooper)

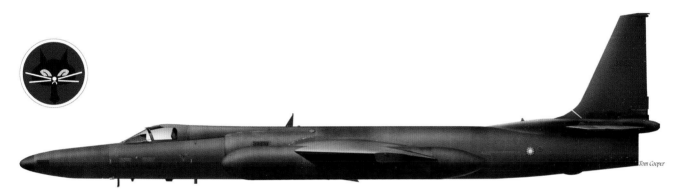

The U-2Rs operated by the 35th Black Cat Squadron, ROCAF, retained their black velvet overall livery, and wore four-digit tail numbers applied in red. In addition to panoramic cameras installed inside the Q-bay, this new variant received a stretched nose with (depending on the mission) either a phased array radar or additional electro-optical cameras (with 16 ports), and two underwing 'superpods' with additional mission-related equipment. Contrary to earlier variants of the U-2 operated by the ROCAF, U-2Rs never flew missions over mainland China: due to political constraints, they were limited to peripheral flights along the edge of the PRC's airspace. Nevertheless, the PLAAF and the PLANAF still launched several intercepts, at least one of which brought one of their MiG-21F-13 close to its target. Inset is shown the famous insignia of the 35th Black Cat Squadron. (Artwork by Tom Cooper)

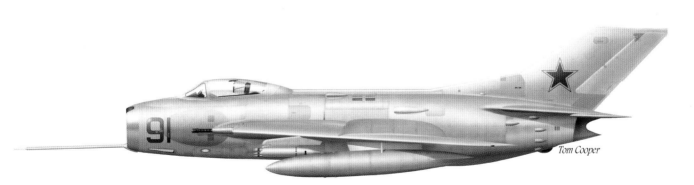

The earliest 'U-2 Hunter' was the MiG-19S: the first of 2nd generation designs by the Mikoyan i Gurevich Design Bureau. As the first supersonic interceptor to enter service with the V-PVO, it was rushed into mass production and thus suffered from poor mechanical reliability. Lacking guided air-to-air missiles, its primary armament consisted of ORO-57K pods for unguided rockets and three internal 30mm cannons. It proved unable to climb to the altitudes at which the RB-57s and U-2s were operating, but was the best available in the 1955-1960 period, and thus saw plenty of action in intercept operations over the USSR. This example served with the 431st IAP based at Afrikanda AB on the Kola Peninsula in the early 1960s. (Artwork by Tom Cooper)

The next variant of the MiG-19 family to enter service and see significant action during various pursuits of U-2s over the USSR was the MiG-19P: a version equipped with the RP-1 Izumrud radar in the nose, and armed with 'only' two NR-30 cannons installed in the wing roots. Like all MiG-19s of the late 1950s, it was painted in two layers of clear lacquer mixed with 5% and 10% aluminium powder, respectively: due to differences in the manufacture of skin panels the aircraft had quite a patchy, though 'highly polished bare metal overall' appearance. Two-digit 'bort' numbers were usually applied in the factory, before the delivery to the operational unit: those of the aircraft assigned to the V-PVO were mostly applied in light blue, with black outline. This example served with the 678th Guards Mixed Test Air Regiment, a Sary-Shagan-based element of the 60th Mixed Test Air Division, in the early 1960s. (Artwork by Tom Cooper)

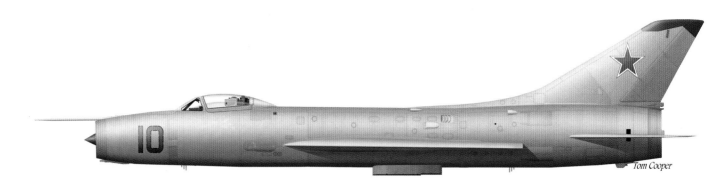

The Sukhoi Su-9 (ASCC/NATO-codename 'Fishpot') was based on the same basic concept as the MiG-21, but much larger and more powerful. Right from the start it was equipped with the R1L (ASCC/NATO-codename 'High Fix') airborne intercept radar and could carry four K-5/RS-2U (ASCC/NATO-codename 'AA-1 Alkali') air-to-air missiles. While a slightly modified example of this 'Defender of the Cities' set a new world record for absolute height on 4 September 1959, reaching 28,852m (94,658ft), the maximum ceiling of the operational variant was 20,000m (66,000ft) – which should have been enough to catch a U-2. The exact bort numbers of the Su-9s flown by Captain Doroshenko on 9 April 1960, and Captain Mientiukov on 1 May 1960 remain unknown, but all the jets of this type were painted in two layers of clear lacquer with, apparently, a slightly higher percentage of aluminium powder than on earlier MiGs, resulting in the colour generally known as 'silver-grey'. (Artwork by Tom Cooper)

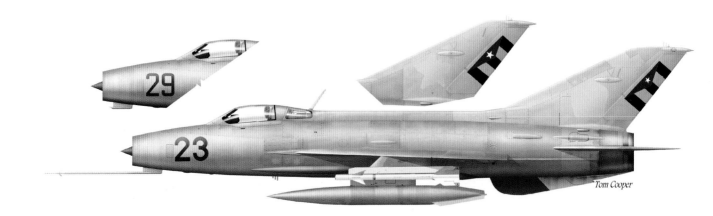

Early Soviet MiG-21s were all painted in the same silver-grey overall as Su-9s. Assigned to the fighter aviation wings of the tactical aviation, they usually wore borts applied in red, which – apparently – were not outlined in black. When deployed to Cuba, the aircraft of the 32nd GIAP (re-designated as the 213th IAP during Operation Anadyr) were left in the same livery, but had their Soviet national insignia crudely overpainted in a light grey colour, and the Cuban national insignia applied, also often quite crudely, on the ruder. Nevertheless, they retained their borts. Principal armament consisted of R-3S missiles. The inset shows details of one of at least two 0-series MiG-21Fs assigned to the 213th IAP (the other was bort 09), both of which retained their narrow-chord fins, even when upgraded to the MiG-21F-13-standard. (Artwork by Tom Cooper)

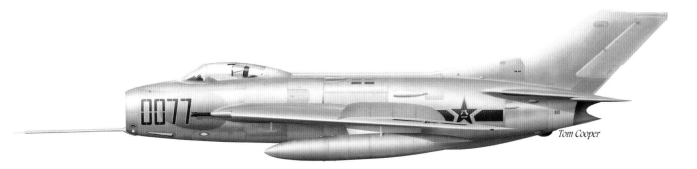

After launching domestic production of the MiG-17F in 1957, Beijing requested the technology transfer for a supersonic fighter from Moscow. In October of the same year, the USSR reacted by granting permission for the sale of the MiG-19S and all the related technical documentation to the PRC. The work on setting up licence production was launched in December 1958, but interrupted due to the first break with the Soviets, prompting the Chinese Communists to launch an indigenous effort to copy the type. Following successful testing, series production of the J-6 – actually an improved variant – was launched in late 1963, and the type eventually entered service with the PLAAF and the PLANAF in huge numbers. Early J-6s still looked very much like the Soviet originals, i.e. were painted in two layers of clear lacquer mixed with aluminium powder: the primary difference was in their four- (later five-) digit serials, and national markings. (Artwork by Tom Cooper)

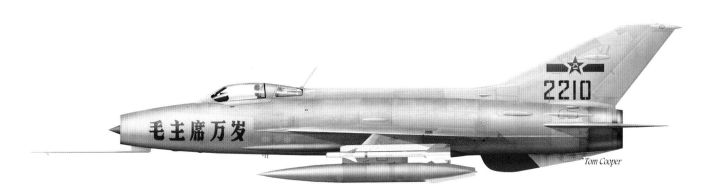

China experienced significant problems with lunching domestic production of the MiG-21F-13 and it seems that most of the early J-7s were actually assembled from MiG-21F-13s delivered from the USSR. This was one of fewer than two dozen MiG-21F-13s that actually entered operational service with PLAAF units in the 1960s. Following the 'norms' from the times of the Cultural Revolution, it was decorated with oversized political slogans on the forward fuselage, while the serial was moved to the base of the fin, and the national marking applied above it. The aircraft was usually armed with a single NR-30 internal cannon installed on the right side of the lower fuselage and a pair of R-3S air-to-air missiles – subsequently replaced by their Chinese copy, the PL-2 (both received the ASCC/NATO-codename 'AA-2 Atoll'). (Artwork by Tom Cooper)

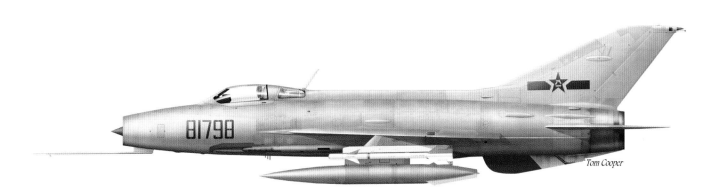

The 'MiG-21' that intercepted the ROCAF U-2R on 29 April 1971 was most likely one of the J-7As of the 9th Naval Aviation Division of the PLANAF: this was the former 9th Fighter Division of the PLAAF, re-assigned to the North Sea Fleet of the PLAN, the 25th Air Regiment of which is known to have operated J-7s and been deployed in the Qingdao area as of the 1970s. The aircraft was left in 'silver-grey' overall, and – in addition to the prominent serial on the forward fuselage – wore the national insignia in six positions, including the 'standard' one, low on the fin. Armament consisted of two Chinese copies of the NR-30, and a pair of PL-2s. (Artwork by Tom Cooper)

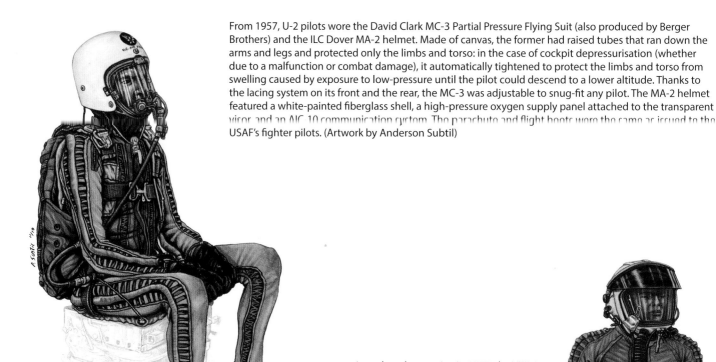

From 1957, U-2 pilots wore the David Clark MC-3 Partial Pressure Flying Suit (also produced by Berger Brothers) and the ILC Dover MA-2 helmet. Made of canvas, the former had raised tubes that ran down the arms and legs and protected only the limbs and torso: in the case of cockpit depressurisation (whether due to a malfunction or combat damage), it automatically tightened to protect the limbs and torso from swelling caused by exposure to low-pressure until the pilot could descend to a lower altitude. Thanks to the lacing system on its front and the rear, the MC-3 was adjustable to snug-fit any pilot. The MA-2 helmet featured a white-painted fiberglass shell, a high-pressure oxygen supply panel attached to the transparent visor, and an AIC-10 communication system. The parachute and flight boots were the same as issued to the USAF's fighter pilots. (Artwork by Anderson Subtil)

Introduced to service in 1957, the VKK-3 Partial Pressure Suit was the Soviet equivalent to the MC-3 developed in the mid-1950s to protect pilots flying MiG-21s and Su-9 at high altitudes. It was a simple design made of canvas, with an H-shaped tube starting at the abdomen and travelling down each leg and arm. The VKK-3 was principally worn in combination with the GSh-4 high-altitude helmet, made of aluminium (the combination of the two was known as the KKO-3). The latter included its own tube for oxygen supply, a communication system, and could – as illustrated here – include a sun visor. Leather gloves and flight boots were the same as issued to all other fighter pilots. (Artwork by Anderson Subtil)

The roomier cockpit of the U-2R enabled the pilots to wear the David Clark S1010 Full Pressure Suit (and later the S1031, similar to the S1030 worn by the crews of the SR-71). This was a fully enclosed, six-layer suit, with harness and flotation systems attached to its vest, which had to be custom-tailored for every pilot. The S1010 included full-length sleeves with metallic rings and a locking mechanism for the gloves on each arm; another ring with a locking mechanism that served as a connecting point for the helmet, at the neck; and it also enclosed the feet at the bottom of the suit's legs. The helmet was made of fiberglass and consisted of two shells, with the inside made of neoprene and grey-coloured rubber. Atop of the transparent visor was the sun visor, which could be raised or lowered by hand. Boots were standard issue but worn 2-2.5 sizes larger than normal to accommodate the feet when the suit was fully inflated. (Artwork by Anderson Subtil)

A well-known photograph of Francis Gary Powers wearing the David Clark MC-3 partial pressure suit, and posing in front of a former U-2A – meanwhile upgraded to the U-2C standard. Notable are the sea blue overall livery of the jet in the background, the short dorsal canoe fairing, and the sugar scoop plate shielding the exhaust from below. (CIA)

Tom Cooper & David Bocquelet

The speartip of the S-75 SAM-system – and the deadly 'Nemesis' of high-flying RB-57s and U-2s in the 1960-1967 period – were the SM-63-I launcher and the V-750V/11D missile, both of which are shown here. Developed by the Central Design Bureau-34 (TsKB-34), the launcher was always painted in dark olive green. Installed on a cruciform base and powered by electric motors, it could traverse for 360° and elevate the launch rail as necessary. Designed by the Fakel Design Bureau (OKB-2), the V-750V/11D missile of the S-75 Dvina system shown here was initially painted in aluminium overall and consisted of two stages: the booster section with big wings at the rear which was ejected four seconds after the launch, at which point the liquid-fuelled sustainer engine of the second stage ignited and carried the missile towards the target. The improved V-750VN/13D missile of the S-75N Desna SAM-system – as used in the shooting down of most of the U-2s lost in the 1960s – was outwardly identical. Examples exported to China seem only to have had approximately 50% of their maintenance and operational-stencils applied in red. (Artwork by Tom Cooper & David Bocquelet)

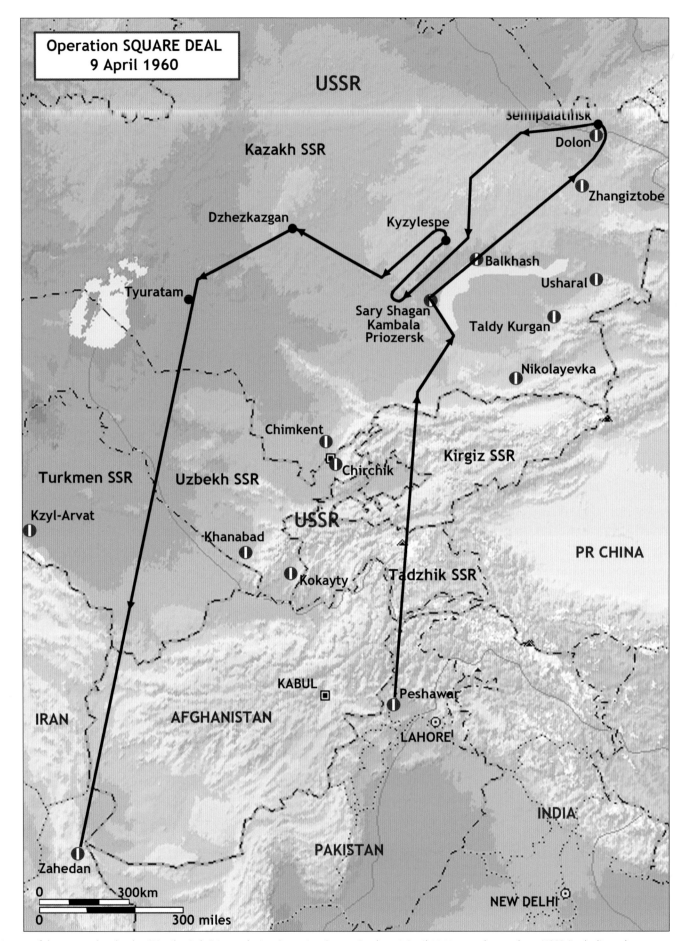

Operation SQUARE DEAL
9 April 1960

USSR

Kazakh SSR

Semipalatinsk

Dolon

Zhangiztobe

Dzhezkazgan

Kyzylespe

Balkhash

Usharal

Tyuratam

Sary Shagan
Kambala
Priozersk

Taldy Kurgan

Nikolayevka

Chimkent

Kirgiz SSR

Turkmen SSR

Uzbek SSR

Chirchik

Kzyl-Arvat

Khanabad

USSR

PR CHINA

Kokayty

Tadzhik SSR

KABUL

Peshawar

IRAN

AFGHANISTAN

LAHORE

INDIA

PAKISTAN

Zahedan

0   300km

0   300 miles

NEW DELHI

A map of the route taken by the CIA-pilot Bob Ericson during Operation Square Deal, on 9 April 1960, over the southern USSR (including what are now Tajikistan, Kirgizstan, Kazakhstan and Uzbekistan). Notably, due to the local terrain, and because the U-2 entered their airspace along a gap in the radar coverage, the Soviets were late in detecting the intruder. Moreover, the nearest air bases (housing units of the 49th Tactical Air Army of the Soviet Air Force), were all much too far away to launch a successful intercept attempt. Ericson thus continued his trip all the way to the Sary Shagari and Kambala-Priozerks complex of airfields (the home bases of the 60th Mixed Test Aviation Division), then to the Dolon AB (a home base of the Soviet Strategic Aviation's Tupolev Tu-95 bombers), and the Baykonour Cosmodrome at Semipalatinsk, before overflying the missile test site at Tyuratam. His overflight thus provoked the longest hunt for the U-2 ever. (Map by Tom Cooper)

flying between Camague and Santa Clara when he spotted what he reported to be a pair of RF-101s. Wasting no time, he moved to attain an advantageous position in the rear hemisphere of the US aircraft – which were actually two Vought RF-8 Crusaders flown by Lieutenant-Commander Tad Riley (US Navy) and Captain Fred Carolan (US Marine Corps), underway on a low-altitude photo-reconnaissance mission. Having realised that they had a MiG on their tails –initially the Americans supposedly saw two 'Fishbeds' – the Crusaders descended to between 10 and 15 metres altitude (about 50 feet) and accelerated, dashing away at a speed of Mach 1.2: this was something no MiG-21 at the time could follow.

False Soviet Claims

Ironically, all of these encounters (and a few others, about which the Soviet fliers did not boast as proudly because these ended with their disadvantage) had one common denominator: none was launched intentionally (for example on the orders of ground control and in reaction to a violation of the Cuban airspace by a US aircraft), and – as far as is known – the pilots of the 213th GIAP were not once scrambled to intercept any of the U-2s passing high above Cuba. Nevertheless, decades later, multiple military aviation historians in the former USSR have claimed that all of the above-mentioned encounters resulted in the *destruction* of the US aircraft in question. Correspondingly, the pilots of the 213th IAP would have shot down a single Voodoo on 18 October, and two Starfighters on 20 and 26 October 1962. Not only have no Soviet pilots ever made a claim of this kind, but they did not fire a single shot during these encounters. Unfortunately, they subsequently found themselves being ridiculed and their credibility questioned – all for, supposedly, their 'fake achievements'.

That said, the Soviet troops deployed to Cuba as of 1962, did fire at least a few shots during the crisis – even if not in the air – but on the ground. Late at night on an unknown date, an unknown person was stopped and challenged by a Soviet guard outside one of the air bases. When the person failed to stop, the guard fired a warning shot and, when this was ignored, another one in the direction of the 'menace hiding in the dark'. The intruder dropped to the ground – only to turn out to be a cow. The net result of this incident was positive – at least from the Soviets point of view: for a few days afterwards, the personnel of the 213th IAP could enjoy some fresh beef.

The Cuban Missile Crisis

The events described so far may convey a false impression that the whole Cuban affair was not much more than a Soviet overseas excursion resulting in some of the 'usual Cold War games'. Nothing could be further from the truth: the situation was very serious to the point of being grave. The United States made it clear that Soviet nuclear missiles right on its doorstep were not acceptable and they would have

to be removed from Cuba in one way or another. At the same time the Cubans, with the Bay of Pigs invasion fresh in their memory, were very nervous, especially that they may not have had the full picture of the developing situation. To what extent they were in the know regarding the ongoing Kennedy–Khrushchev negotiations can be a matter of dispute. According to Aleksandr Alekseyev, contemporary Soviet Ambassador to Havana, he briefed the country's leader on each exchange of massages between Moscow and Washington, but Castro may have been in the dark, so to speak. This is so for it remains doubtful if the ambassador – considering his rank and posting as well as objective technical difficulties – would have received detailed information about the Kennedy–Khrushchev correspondence. Soviet military personnel on the island also felt a great strain for they clearly understood that they were at the very front line of the Cold War, which could turn 'hot' at any moment. To complicate matters even more, Moscow kept them in the dark about how the situation was developing, which – amongst others – is best illustrated by the fact that the Soviets deployed to Cuba considered the US-run radio station Voice of America to be one of their best sources of information. To make matters worse, the instructions provided to their commanders were often vague. For example, the deployment of weapons was granted only in the case of 'manifested attack' – while the rules of engagement lacked a detailed definition of what could be considered as such: interceptor-pilots thus did not know whether they should attack incoming aircraft while these were still approaching, or only once these had actually deployed bombs, rockets, or their cannons. Such lack of clarity was not accidental, but resulted from what can be defined as the 'Soviet political culture': on one hand Moscow wanted to maintain tight control over unfolding events, but on the other the decision-makers in the Soviet capital were keen to have convenient scapegoats in case anything went wrong. Tight control required issuing instructions with many restrictions, while the latter option demanded purposeful vagueness, so as to enable blaming the people

A Cuban anti-aircraft-artillery site outside San Cristobal, photographed by a low-flying US reconnaissance jet on 26 October, while opening fire. Castro's conviction that a war with the USA was not only imminent, but unavoidable, exercised a strong influence upon Grechko's decision to activate the V-PVO's SAM-sites on Cuba and open fire the following day. (NSA)

The S-75 SAM-site of the V-PVO outside Banes, on Cuba, as photographed by a low-flying US reconnaissance aircraft. Notable are the Fan Song radar, the command post and support equipment in the centre, four launchers with missiles in their positions, and three reloads on their trails on the left side. (USAF)

A Soviet FKR-1 Meteor cruise missile site deployed outside Banes, as seen on a photograph taken by one of the CIA's U-2s. (NSA)

Missile Air Defence Division had constructed and deployed 24 SAM-sites. However, not one of all these was ever activated. Indeed, multiple missions by Boeing RB-47Hs of the 55th Strategic Reconnaissance Wing, not to mention the US Navy's 'technical research ship' USS *Oxford* (AGTR-1) – a vessel well-equipped for ELINT and SIGINT gathering – could not even collect enough intelligence to confirm that they had been integrated into an air defence system. In other words: Soviet S-75s were in Cuba, but 'zip lip'. Despite all the overflights by US reconnaissance aircraft, they never powered up their radars, let alone opened fire.

The Americans were not the only ones wondering about this behaviour. Late in the evening of 26 October, Fidel Castro visited the Soviet HQ at El Chico: considering the situation and near-constant violations of Cuban airspace by US aircraft, and the threat of an invasion, he demanded that the Soviets activate their air defences: to open fire – in the same fashion as he had already issued an order for the air defences of the Cuban armed forces to open fire – at the intruders. Having no such orders from Moscow, the Soviets proved reluctant. Nevertheless, they were eventually to bow to Castro's demands. Early on the morning of 27 October, their SAM-sites powered up their radars, de-facto establishing a 'no-go' zone over Cuba for high-flying US aircraft. The RB-47Hs and USS *Oxford* took a few hours to detect and confirm this important development, and then to report it to Washington. By then, it was too late.

in theatre for 'failing to act according to orders'. Considering this, it is obvious how difficult it was for the Soviet commanders in Cuba to perform their duties and make the proper decisions.

Target 33

The situation was not the least pleasant for the US side either – especially not for the U-2 pilots involved. The primary issue was the presence of the Soviet S-75 SAM-sites: their deployment had been detected by a CIA U-2 mission on 29 August. The Americans also had little problem in finding out that by 26 October 1962 the personnel of the 11th

Meanwhile, preparations for another day of intensive flying activity were taking place across the Florida Strait. Originally, as many as four U-2 missions were planned for 27 October, but in the end only a single U-2 operated by the USAF, with Major Rudolf Anderson at the controls, received the order to make an overflight from McCoy AFB, while equipped with reconnaissance cameras and SIGINT-gathering systems. Since by the time of his take-off nobody in the USA had issued any warnings about the activation of Soviet S-75 SAM-sites on Cuba, Anderson was totally oblivious to the mortal danger he was about to confront.[6]

Of course, as soon as the USAF U-2 approached Cuban airspace it was detected and tracked by Soviet radars and assigned the designation 'Target 33'. Together with their commanders, the operators nervously monitored the aircraft's progress as it crossed the island on a north-west to south-east axis, all the time feeding related reports to several S-75 SAM-sites that were now on full combat alert. Right from the start, the Soviets knew that the high-flying intruder was neither 'innocent', nor alone. Their work in turn was still tracked by one of the RB-47Hs of the 55th SRW and by the crew of USS *Oxford*. Just as the presence of the U-2 and the RB-47H did not escape the attention of Soviet radar operators, so also the activity of their radars did not escape the attention of US operators: however, the latter were unable to communicate directly to Anderson, and warn him in time.[7]

Initially at least, the Deputy Commander of the Soviet Forces on Cuba, General Leonid Garbuz and the Deputy Commander Air Defence, General Stepan Grechko were debating how to handle the situation. They wanted the overall Commander of the Soviet Forces on Cuba, General Issa Pliyev, to make the decision about what to do – or not – with Target 33. However, it proved impossible to get hold of Pliyev, because he was absent – or at least that is what his aide-de-camp stated. Pliyev is known to have suffered serious health problems related to his kidneys and was thus most likely incapacitated.

Meanwhile, Anderson steered his U-2 over Guantanamo Bay before continuing in a western direction – a fact that became crucial in what happened next. This brought him on a course directly over a Soviet unit equipped with FKR-1 Meteor (ASCC/NATO-codename 'SSC-2 Salish') cruise missiles, deployed outside the village of Filipinas. The FKR-1 missiles deployed there were equipped with 12 kiloton nuclear warheads and meant to 'neutralize' the US base at Guantanamo in the case of an invasion. Because the missiles were moved into this position during the night from 26 to 27 October, their presence could not have been revealed by earlier US reconnaissance missions and therefore they were still a secret from the Americans (their discovery came about on 28 October, but they were mistaken for anti-ship missiles). The fact that Major Anderson overflew the area in question was arguably one of the main reasons behind the decision

of two Soviet deputy commanders to order their S-75 units to open fire and shoot down the U-2.

Having flown over Guantanamo, Anderson turned in a north-westerly direction, actually intending to overfly the island and then continue straight back to the USA. His progress was constantly monitored by Soviet radars, and Garbuz and Grechko now understood that the time had come to decide and to act. Unable to reach their superior commander, they took the responsibility upon themselves: the two Soviet generals agreed to order the downing of Target 33.

Tragic Fate of Major Anderson

The events then moved very quickly: General Grechko issued the order to destroy the U-2 via telephone to the CO of the 11th AD Division, Colonel Georgi Voronkov. The latter repeated the order to his superior (it was a standard procedure for the recipient to repeat the order received so as to ensure to his superior that it was clearly understood), and then forwarded it to the CO of the 507th AD Regiment, Guseinov, who in turn did the same passing down the order to Major Ivan Gerchenkov, the commander of the regiment's 1st Battalion. The later was located in the vicinity of the town of Banes in Oriente province. Its radar van was crewed – besides Major Gerchenkov who was supervising the actions of his subordinates – by Vasily Gorshakov, Alexander Ryapenko (the latter was the guidance officer) and several others, in accordance with related procedures. The American aircraft, which was flying at an altitude of 22,000m, was engaged at a range of 12km. While two of the three missiles fired by the Soviets detonated underneath and behind the target, the third exploded above it, spraying the U-2 with shrapnel: one piece penetrated not only the cockpit, but also the protective suit of Major Anderson, thus instantly decompressing both. The disabled pilot promptly lost control of his disintegrating aircraft, the wreckage of which came down near the village of Veguitas, with pilot's body still strapped to his ejection seat. Unsurprisingly, yet tragically, there was no way for Anderson to survive this catastrophe. Gerchenkov reported up the chain of command that he had fulfilled his task – i.e. to have shot down the US aircraft – at 10:19hrs local time.

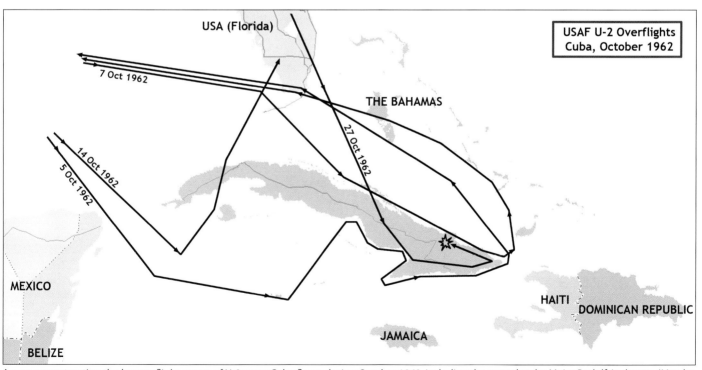

A map reconstructing the known flight routes of U-2s over Cuba flown during October 1962, including the one taken by Major Rudolf Anderson. (Map by Tom Cooper)

Wreckage of Major Anderson's U-2, as found by Cuban troops. Notable is the large service title, reading 'U. S. Air Force', applied in white (for details on Anderson's jet, see the colour section). (TASS, via Albert Grandolini)

Curious villagers quickly flocked to the crash site and Cuban military personnel also appeared at the scene. In no time, Cuban radio – soon to be followed by the press – boasted of a great victory over the 'Yankee imperialists'. Understandably, the mood across the Florida Strait was not ecstatic. The news of the U-2's downing reached Washington just as President Kennedy was holding another meeting in the White House. Beforehand the US president and his closest aides had agreed that if an American aircraft was shot down the US would attack Cuba. Fortunately, they changed their mind, not least because they thought that the decision to fire on US aircraft was not a deliberate provocation by Moscow, but one that was made locally. With hindsight, it is on record that this assessment was correct. The action by Major Gerchenkov, and the decisions by Grechkov and Garbuz thus did not result in the Third World War.

Aurora Borealis

Despite Kennedy's decision not to retaliate to the downing of Major Anderson's U-2, the hunt went on. Indeed, only hours later, the USA found themselves on the verge of losing another aircraft over Cuba. While Cuban forces had no means to engage high-flying targets in 1962, they were meanwhile lavishly supplied with anti-aircraft machineguns and light cannons, and these were no empty threat vis-à-vis low-flying US aircraft. This became obvious when a pair of US Navy RF-8 Crusaders underway on a low-altitude reconnaissance mission was hit by these, and one of the two pilots proved rather lucky to bring his badly-damaged bird safely back to base. However, because no loss of life occurred, the White House chose to ignore this 'incident', and it had no impact upon the subsequent developments. This was even more so because the Soviet Ambassador in Havana, Alekseyev, subsequently exercised severe pressure upon Castro to order his air defences not to shoot at US aircraft – and thus avoid

While, sadly, no photographs of Soviet interceptors – or their pilots – involved in the hunt for the USAF U-2 that inadvertently penetrated Soviet airspace on 27 October 1962 are available, those of the U-2 pilot are: this is Captain Charles Maultsby. (USAF)

Many of the U-2s flown by the USAF of the early 1960s were early models, and still left unpainted, as was the U-2A, USAF FY-serial number 56-713, flown by Maultsby during this mission over the Arctic on 27 October 1962. (USAF)

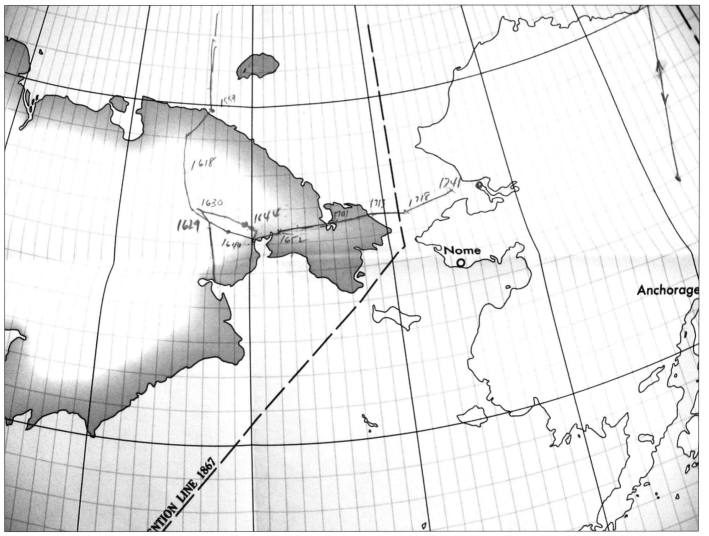

A map reconstructing the route flown by Captain Charles Maultsby on 27 October 1962, found by Washington Post reporter Michael Dobbs in the records of the State Department Executive Secretariat at the National Archives. (NSA)

aggravating the already exceptionally high tensions.[8]

Moreover, the fateful 27 October 1962 was still not over. Indeed, it was in the middle of this drama that the situation nearly exploded because of developments half the world away. Entirely unrelated to the developments in and around Cuba, Captain Charles W Maultsby of the USAF took off from Alaska in a U-2 to fly an air-sampling mission over the Arctic.[9]

High above the North Pole, the US pilot then made a navigational error due to the unreliability of the compass in that part of the world, and the inability to take a proper celestial navigation fix because of the Aurora Borealis (northern lights). As a result, he strayed off course and well inside Soviet airspace. Of course, the V-PVO did not miss the intrusion. On the contrary, it detected it and promptly scrambled interceptors from at least two units of the Far Eastern Military District. A pair of MiGs are known to have launched from Pewek AB, off the northern coast of Chukotka, and they traced the U-2 as it flew south over Soviet territory. Another pair of MiGs was then scrambled from Anadyr AB on the southern coast of Chukotka and made an attempted intercept about 30 minutes later. Once again, they failed to catch the intruder for the same reason as so many times before and after: because it flew too high.

As the latter pair of V-PVO interceptors followed Maultsby's U-2 in the direction of the USA, and alerted by intercepted Soviet radio communication, the Alaska Air Defense Command then scrambled a pair of Convair F-102A Delta Dagger interceptors armed with two GAR-11 (later AIM-26) Falcon air-to-air missiles each: such missiles were armed with nuclear warheads.[10]

As 'interesting' as an air combat involving the use of nuclear-tipped air-to-air missiles might appear, fortunately, this was avoided. Indeed, there was no need for the American fighters to intervene, because the Soviet interceptors could not reach the intruder. Thus, Captain Maultsby exited Soviet air space unmolested, even if now out of fuel. He was able to glide for nearly an hour before landing at Kotzebue, on the western tip of Alaska. As an interesting side note: his flight of 10 hours and 25 minutes was the longest ever recorded by any U-2.

Fortunately, the whole incident had no repercussions other than wrecking the already strained nerves of all those involved, as illustrated by the un-presidential yet – all things considered – understandable remark by President Kennedy that, '…there's always some son of a bitch who doesn't get the word…'.

Resumé

Looking back at the events described above it can be stated that, on one hand, the shooting down of a reconnaissance aircraft was almost a 'typical' Cold War incident; on the other, it was unique not only because every case is unique but, also because of the circumstances during the Cuban Missile Crisis in general. Namely it was one of those situations when the Cold War could have turned really hot with an exchange of nuclear missiles between the superpowers a realistic possibility. This particular incident illustrates well the various dangers, difficulties

A USAF-operated U-2C preparing for take-off in the mid-1960s, by when most of the aircraft were painted in blue overall, and many had received canoe-shaped fairings with additional reconnaissance equipment atop the rear fuselage. (USAF)

and problems faced by all sides: the assessing of what was actually going on, what the other side's intentions were, what to do in case of sudden developments, how do deal with a lack of vital information and how to interpret instructions that were either vague or did not fit the circumstances just to name a few. Fortunately, the parties involved were able to restrain themselves and the second US-operated U-2 to be shot down by Soviet-operated SAMs thus remained an isolated incident, which did not result in an escalation. Otherwise, it is rather unlikely that any books like this one would have ever been written.

Of course, the resulting incidents caused entirely different reactions in the East and the West. The Soviets deployed to Cuba, while not gleeful, felt a sense of having done a good job for they had shot down an aircraft, and that was, after all, their 'field of business'. Colonel Voronkov visited the SAM site to congratulate Gerchenkov and his men. Perhaps a little surprisingly, the whole affair made almost no impression in Moscow. The Soviet Minister of Defence, Marshal Rodion Malinovski, laconically remarked that it was done a little too early. A similar reaction was ascribed to Khrushchev, too. Arguably the Soviet leadership was preoccupied with the ongoing negotiations and since this incident did not derail them it did not warrant much attention.

No doubt, there were similar feelings on the Western side of the tribune – though also that the entire world was lucky to avoid the ultimate confrontation. Once the Cuban Missile Crisis ended with the withdrawal of Soviet ballistic missiles armed with nuclear warheads (for its part the USA agreed to remove similar missiles deployed in

Turkey and Italy), Major Rudolf Anderson's body was returned to the United States and laid to rest on 6 November at Woodlawn Memorial Park. The pilot who paid the ultimate price for the superpowers' brinkmanship, deserves not to be forgotten, along with all the other victims of the Cold War. The wreckage of his aircraft remains on display at the Museum of the Revolution in Havana and a few parts are on display at the Playa Girón Museum – even if not related to the earlier 'Bay of Pigs' invasion.

That said, the U-2 continued flying reconnaissance operations at least 'close' to Cuba. Indeed, while avoiding a direct confrontation with their 'nemesis', the S-75 SAM-system and its variants, the type thus became involved in another fatal incident in this part of the world. On 28 July 1966, Captain Robert Hickman took off from Barkasdale AFB in Louisiana to make one of the regular 'overflights' of the island. Contrary to earlier times, he was not supposed to make an overflight but was explicitly ordered not to violate Cuban airspace. Unfortunately, due to the failure of the aircraft's oxygen supply system (as was subsequently determined), the pilot suffered hypoxia and his U-2 continued on directly for Cuba. In order to avoid an incident, the US Navy then scrambled two McDonnell Douglas F-4 Phantom II interceptors from NAS Key West, in Florida, to shoot the aircraft down. Remarkably, this proved a task too much even for the powerful Phantom. Therefore, the U-2 overflew the Caribbean island – without provoking any kind of reaction from the Cubans: it flew on until running out of fuel and crashing over Bolivia, where Captain Hickman's body was recovered from the wreckage.[11]

8
ASIAN ALTERCATIONS

After the downing of Francis Gary Powers over Sverdlovsk, and in the aftermath of Major Rudolf Anderson's tragic loss over Cuba, the operations of the U-2s would never be the same again. The two incidents made it crystal clear that manned reconnaissance flights deep over Soviet airspace were much too dangerous. Unsurprisingly, these were now discontinued without replacement. That said, technically speaking, they were 'merely halted' – on the order of President Eisenhower, and upheld by his successor, Kennedy. Although there were voices demanding the resumption of U-2 overflights, nobody in the USA had the authorisation to lift or countermand such an order, and thus they were never re-launched.[1]

However, this did not mean that the U-2 was out of business. Quite

on the contrary: the type was to see much more action, 'somewhere else' – and thus to prompt many more hunts.

Indeed, US experiences of the 1960-1962 period resulted in U-2-operations being much more formalised. Henceforth, every single mission was preceded by a detailed request for permission, which was not only expected to provide a justification, but also to cover possible emergencies and other related issues. Moreover, aerial intelligence gathering and reconnaissance activity had to be conducted with much better-coordination between the CIA and the USAF. While not removed from such activities, the CIA eventually saw its role in airborne operations being reduced to that of doing a favour for the USAF and had its detachments withdrawn from bases abroad.[2]

That said, the CIA did remain involved in U-2 operations – 'somewhere else': the theatre of operations in question was the People's Republic of China. As already mentioned, China was regularly reconnoitred from the air by the USA and by the Republic of China, i.e. former Chinese Nationalists that found refuge on Taiwan. Indeed, the Agency was constantly supplying additional aircraft and equipment to the ROCAF – also because the cooperation with the Chinese Nationalists offering it a sort of 'advantage': no US citizens were required to fly over mainland China, and thus the 'occasional loss' of one or the other could not derail the efforts to continue the overflights. Thus, even before the ROCAF lost its two RB-57s over the PRC, the idea came into being to provide the Taiwanese

A top-view of a ROCAF-operated U-2. (ROCAF)

with the most advanced high-altitude reconnaissance available in those days, the U-2.[3]

As previously mentioned, the idea of having non-US pilots fly the U-2 was not new, but was indeed preferred for particularly dangerous undertakings – foremost because it enabled Washington the element of plausible deniability. Due to a number of factors nothing came out of it early on, and although some British pilots would fly at least a few of operational U-2-sorties, no such aircraft were transferred to the RAF. In the case of Taiwan, Washington and Langley were ready to make an exception. This is how it happened that a group of Taiwanese pilots were sent to Laughlin Air Force Base (AFB) in Texas, for conversion training on the U-2. Amongst them was Major Hua His-chun (Mike Hua) who also experienced the first mishap with the new type. While running a nocturnal navigation sortie at 70,000ft on 3 August 1959 his aircraft suffered an engine flame-out. In turn, the loss of power resulted in the disengagement of the autopilot and denied the pilot the use of the landing gear: this would not extend. Hua thus had to glide and belly-land the aircraft. After a longer search, he finally spotted the runway lights of Cortez Airfield in Colorado. Hua made an almost perfect belly landing: the aircraft skidded off the runway and came to rest in the grass, sustaining repairable damage. The Taiwanese pilot was subsequently awarded the Distinguished Flying Cross for his achievement.[4]

Aside of such mishaps, the training of ROCAF pilots in the USA was as productive as it could be and soon enough the question was what to do with them. The CIA had two alternatives: have an American detachment on Taiwan to operate U-2s with local pilots, or hand them over to the ROCAF. Eventually, a combination of both options was chosen, because – in the case of a loss over mainland China – it provided the option of complete deniability for the USA. On 26 August 1960, President Eisenhower thus approved the hand-over of U-2s to Taiwan: the aircraft were to be flown by the ROCAF, but operated on behalf of the CIA, which was also to help with the maintenance (the aircraft were actually to be maintained by Lockheed's technicians contracted by the Agency), select their objectives and plan missions,

and to have exclusive access to the intelligence collected. Indeed, the latter was originally not even shared with the Taiwanese government or authorities.

The first U-2s were delivered to Taiwan on 14 December 1961, and formed the nucleus of the newly-established 35th Black Cat Squadron, based at Taoyuan AB. From the CIA's standpoint, the unit was designated Detachment H – and was always referred to under this designation in all the related documentation. As this – truly 'joint' – operation began picking pace, the 35th Squadron suffered its next mishap, once again proving how dangerous to fly the early U-2s were. On 19 March 1961, the aircraft piloted by Yaohua Chih veered off the runway, crashed and caught fire, killing its sole occupant.

Project TACKLE

Having received approval from the highest levels in Washington, U-2 overflights of mainland China commenced on 12 January 1962 and were run within Project TACKLE (other cryptonyms would also be used subsequently). On that day a U-2 with Chen Huai-sheng (Huai Chen) at the controls overflew the missile-testing range at Shuangchengzi. Unfortunately, due to a navigational error – or faulty maps – the aircraft was poorly positioned: instead of taking the desired vertical photographs it took only oblique photographs of the objective.

Of course, additional missions were flown before long, and then over other installations, facilities, and major military bases. Initially, the resulting film was then flown from Taiwan to the US bases at Okinawa or Guam for development and processing, and the Americans never shared any of the missions' results. It was only years later that they agreed to share some, and then complete sets, of the resulting photographs, and it took even longer until Taiwan was assisted in setting up its own photo-development and interpretation unit at Taoyuan AB.

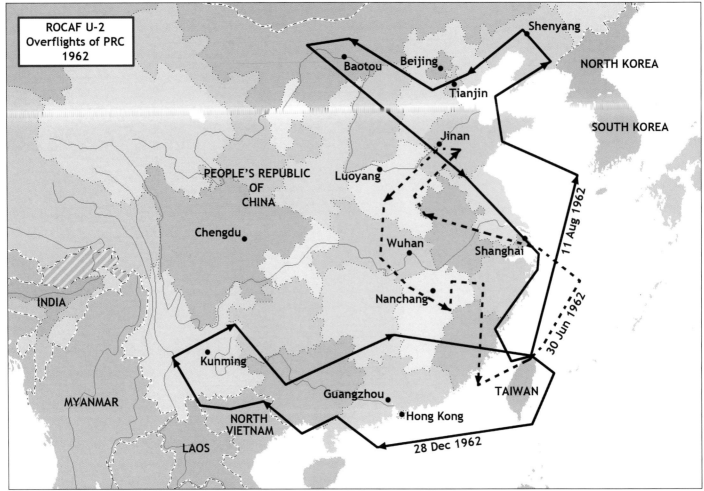

A map showing some of the overflights of the PRC made by U-2s of 35th Black Cat Squadron, ROCAF, in 1962. (Map by Tom Cooper)

Unwelcome Guests

Constantly on alert because of countless other intrusions into its airspace – foremost by low-flying ROCAF transports and patrol aircraft deploying agents deep inside the mainland by night – the PLAAF was quick in realising that it was frequently visited by 'uninvited guests', and promptly decided to counter these. Indeed, nearly every single Taiwanese overflight was 'followed' by MiG-17s and then MiG-19s, the pilots of which were tracking the intruders: pilots of the Black Cat Squadron could frequently see small silver dots at the head of a long white condensation trail in their main sights. However, the interceptors in service with the PLAAF and the PLANAF at the time lacked the capability to climb to the altitude where they could successfully intercept the U-2. At most, they could only hope that some sort of a malfunction might force the U-2s to descend. Whether by sheer luck, or because there were no such mishaps, the Taiwanese were never forced to fly lower than 60,000ft (18,288m).

However, the PLA meanwhile had all of its first few SAM-units in an operational condition, and two of these had had their first taste of combat. Indeed, their commanders knew how to deal with high-altitude targets. Their only problem was the relatively limited range of their missiles: this required the U-2 to almost directly overfly their position in order to be engaged. Effectively, this meant that as long as a U-2 did not overfly a location defended by the SAMs it could still operate well inside Chinese airspace with impunity. In a nutshell, the Chinese had similar problems dealing with the U-2 as the Soviets had at earlier times; contrary to the Soviets, they eventually proved capable of tackling the issue.

In order to be able to counter the aerial incursions with the means available – in particular their S-75s – the Chinese tried to detect the incoming intruders at the earliest possible point in time, so as to reposition their air defence assets correspondingly. After studying the U-2 flight patterns they concluded that Nanchang was the place most likely to be paid a "visit" by the elusive aerial intruders. Accordingly, S-75s were deployed there and the only thing left to do was to wait. On at least two occasions, a ROCAF U-2 was detected approaching Nanchang, but every time the jet would turn away for one or the other reason. Nevertheless, the proverbial Chinese patience paid off on 9 September 1962.

It was on this date that the U-2 'Article 387', piloted by Chen Huai-sheng (the same man who flew the first Taiwanese U-2 mission over mainland China), did not turn away, but flew straight into the range of S-75s operated by the 2nd Surface-to-Air Guided Missile Battalion. The commander of the latter unit, Yue Zhenhua, was already experienced from his first 'kill' against an RB-57, and thus almost routinely controlling the work of his team. Once again, his missiles worked as advertised, and a salvo of three resulted in the downing of the U-2. Badly wounded, Chen Huai-sheng was found still alive: alas, he succumbed to his injuries while being treated in a nearby hospital.

While the CIA this time acknowledged the loss of the precious reconnaissance aircraft, for reasons that are unclear, the Americans strongly distorted the details. Not only that they reported that the aircraft had already disappeared in August 1962, but they also credited its demise to an engine flame-out. Supposedly, this would have forced the pilot to descend, where he was shot down by interceptors using air-to-air missiles – a weapons configuration that was not in service in China at the time. Finally, the Americans said that the pilot ejected safely and was captured. Virtually all of this account was wrong: indeed, interceptors armed with air-to-air missiles were not even available in China at the time. The sole exception was the fact that the pilot survived the downing and, at least for a short while, fell into Chinese hands.[5]

As a result of this loss, President Kennedy ordered a general stand-down of all overflights of mainland China. As so often, this was a short-lived decision: the demand for intelligence was meanwhile much too great. Unsurprisingly, overflights resumed already by December 1962, even if they were re-directed over the southern PRC, where there were fewer radars and SAM-sites. Moreover, the Taiwanese U-2s were occasionally flown by US pilots for operations elsewhere over Asia – always well away from China – and, sometimes, they would be flown by Taiwanese pilots from US bases away from the island.

The Deadly Game of Cat and Mouse

While the first few overflights undertaken after the resumption of ROCAF U-2 operations over the PRC were still undertaken in a rather cautious, indeed limited, fashion, before long they began reaching ever deeper into Chinese airspace. Obviously, this was extremely hazardous, but steps were already taken to alleviate the threat of S-75s through the installation of advanced self-protection systems.

The Soviet-made S-75 system was as close to a sort of 'Wunderwaffe' as it can get in real life, and it caused a number of U-2 losses over time. However, precisely this prompted the Americans to launch multiple research projects all aimed to develop electronic countermeasures (ECM) against it. Indeed, the U-2s of the 35th Squadron were soon outfitted with an electronic warfare (EW) suite that warned the pilot whenever his aircraft was tracked by an early warning radar, and especially if it was tracked by the Fan Song fire-control radar of the S-75 system. Although slightly downgraded in comparison to similar systems meanwhile installed in US-operated aircraft (the reason was that the Americans did not want to reveal their most sensitive equipment to the Chinese, in the case of one of the aircraft being shot down), this was at least sufficient to enable the pilots of 35th Squadron to take timely evasive action. The fact was that the original S-75 was developed with targeting high-flying, but non-manoeuvring, targets in mind: if the target flew any kind of turns – even two minor ones were sufficient – it was almost certain to miss. Similarly, a sudden dive would do the trick of dogging an incoming missile, even if the frail structure of the U-2 was anything other than suitable for performing such a manoeuvre: indeed, several aircraft crashed after disintegrating because their pilots overstressed the airframe in a turn.

Solution for the Manoeuvring Problem

After the Taiwanese U-2s managed to avoid being hit by surface-to-air missiles launched against them on several occasions the Chinese realised that they must be equipped with some sort of electronic countermeasure device. While for obvious reasons its workings remained a mystery, the Chinese concluded that the best way to deal with it would be to shorten the time frame of the engagement so as to give the U-2 pilots as little warning as possible and consequently little time to initiate evasive action. Since Soviet tactical procedures were rigid and time consuming it proved possible to shorten the engagement sequence considerably. In addition, a SAM battery's engagement radar would be activated only if the intended target was well within range.

As the overflights continued it was only a matter of time before the PLA had the opportunity to test the idea practically. On 1 November 1963, the U-2 'Article 355', piloted by Yeh Chang-di (Robin Yeh) was over Jiangxi province when it was suddenly struck by a salvo of three missiles. The 2nd Surface-to-Air Guided Missile Battalion was waiting in ambush and its CO, Yue Zhenhua, ordered the target to be engaged according to the new tactical concept. Within just eight seconds, the Taiwanese pilot found himself outside his disintegrating aircraft's cockpit, with no chance to do anything but regain his senses, wait for his parachute to deploy, and then float down. His problems had only begun, when shortly after he was promptly arrested by the People's Militia.

The wreckage of the downed U-2 'Article 355' was collected by the PLA and carefully examined. Its radar warning receiver (RWR) especially provided highly valuable intelligence to the Chinese: after analysing it, they decided to start making use of alternating frequencies when tracking and engaging a target, so as to 'confuse' the ECM-system carried by the ROCAF aircraft. Moreover, the Chinese concluded that the Taiwanese U-2s were meanwhile equipped with the Birdwatch system that was monitoring their flight data and the RWR and automatically transmitting these to the ground base.

The loss incurred resulted in a stand-down of overflights of mainland China which lasted for almost five months. However, any losses suffered could not stop the overflights for long: the Vietnam War was heating up and the US intelligence services had a crucial – and urgent – interest in monitoring not only the Chinese progress in regards of nuclear weapons, but also the Communist supply lines through the PRC. Therefore, the ROCAF U-2s had to return to the skies over the mainland China.

The inevitable happened again. On 7 June 1964, the U-2 'Article 362' piloted by Lee Nan-ping (Terry Lee) was on a mission of reconnoitring North Vietnamese supply lines passing through China, when his aircraft was ambushed by SA-2s and shot down over Fujian Province. Once again, this was the work of the 2nd Surface-to-Air Guided Missile Battalion, whose commander Yue Zhenhua had thus scored a total of four kills against high-flying ROCAF aircraft. Indeed, the operation that resulted in the destruction of Lee Nan-ping's U-2 was a classic SAM-ambush, thoroughly tested before Yue Zhenhua's unit was deployed into the area of Taiwanese interest – and always under conditions of utmost secrecy. The PLA's commander patiently waited until his target was certain to enter the no-escape zone of his missiles, then quickly activated the Fan Song radar of his SAM-site before firing the usual salvo of three. The ambush worked as planned: Lee Nan-ping's aircraft was promptly shot down and crashed. The pilot's body was found within the wreckage: according to the mainland Chinese sources, he had no chance of saving himself because his ejection seat was not armed.

The Almost SAM-Ace

Every single downing of a U-2 was much celebrated on mainland China, where 'victories over the imperialists' were explained as power-demonstrations: according to the official lines, they had shown that the PRC was capable of defending itself against violent foreign invasions that ruined the country in earlier centuries and left it in a state of deep trauma – one that could only be healed if it was visibly asserting itself against foreign influence. For this reason, the PLA was extremely proud to put the wreckage of every downed U-2 on public display – and anybody bringing a piece of wreckage was honoured. Moreover, on 6 June 1964, the PLA's 2nd Surface-to-Air Guided Missile Battalion was awarded the title of Heroic Battalion, and on 23 July its personnel were received by Chairman Mao himself. For his role as the unit's commander, Yue Zhenhua was promoted to the rank of a full colonel, thus becoming the highest-ranking officer of the PLA to serve in the capacity of a battalion commander. With four 'kills' to his credit – three of which were U-2s – he was just one success short of becoming a true 'SAM ace' and, until the massive air-to-ground battles of the wars in Vietnam, and the Middle East fought in 1967-

The PLA still had only a very limited stock of V-750 missiles as of 1962, and the crews of its four operational S-75 SAM-sites had to be exceptionally cautious when actually firing these. Perhaps precisely for this reason, they proved highly effective in targeting the ROCAF's U-2s. This is another photograph of an early Chinese S-75 SAM-system in position. Notable is the lack of earthen walls around the launchers: there was no threat of a Taiwanese counterattack, and the typical 'star-shell' construction of an S-75-site was likely to alert the ROCAF-pilots to the presence of the weapon system. (Albert Grandolini Collection)

1973, he – unquestionably – possessed the most expertise in operating surface-to-air missiles against real aircraft. Indeed, Yue Zhenhua was also the first to ever deploy the S-75 SAM-system in actual combat, and his feats were not to be repeated by anybody. As such, there was certainly a reason for him to go down in the annals of aerial warfare.

The shoot-down of the ROCAF U-2 in June 1964 resulted in another suspension of overflights of mainland China. The rank and file of the 35th 'Black Cat' Squadron was meanwhile badly depleted, left with less than a handful of operational aircraft, and even fewer pilots qualified to fly them. The situation reached the point at which the suggestion emerged to employ US-citizens, civilian CIA pilots. Such a risky solution was abandoned: indeed, all concerns were put aside, and the Taiwanese operations over the PRC once again resumed after only a few months.

The next overflight took place on 31 October 1964, and was quickly followed by additional missions, during which the U-2s deployed their new ECM-systems including active electronic countermeasures. While initially effective, this measure proved insufficient. Indeed, two additional reconnaissance aircraft were soon shot down. On 10 January 1965, the U-2 'Article 358' (coded 3512) was shot down over inner Mongolia by a salvo of missiles fired by the 1st Guided Surface-to-Air Missile Battalion of the PLA. It's pilot, Chang Li yi (Jack Chang) survived the ordeal of ejecting from an altitude of 22,000 metres to become the second aviator of the 35th 'Black Cat' Squadron to spend years in captivity: he was released only on 10 November 1982.

The Indian Interlude

American high-altitude reconnaissance aircraft, as well as Soviet surface-to-air missiles were some of the most-advanced technology and weaponry in the world-wide arsenals of their time: they provided their users with seemingly unreachable capabilities in the fields of aerial reconnaissance and air defence, respectively. Unsurprisingly, both superpowers experienced lots of demand for such equipment from their allies and, sometimes, they proved ready to provide. This is how India and Pakistan experienced their episode in the hunt for high-altitude reconnaissance aircraft.[6]

Far from being anything like an 'extension' of the Cold War, or even a conflict between the proxies, the arch-rivalry and armed conflict between India and Pakistan were strongly influenced by the global developments. As already mentioned, the CIA began using airfields in northern Pakistan for operations over the USSR and then the PRC during the late 1950s. Indeed, Francis Powers took off for his ill-fated mission on 1 May 1960 from Peshawar. However, unlike Taiwan, the CIA never found a reason to provide U-2s to Pakistan, nor would it ever let any Pakistani pilots fly the type. Instead, when the question was that of providing the country with an aircraft capable of flying high-altitude reconnaissance missions to collect samples after Chinese nuclear tests, the agency decided to furnish two RB-57Fs within the terms of Operation Little Cloud in 1963. Apart from being equipped with big turbofan engines with more than double the thrust of their original Wright J-65 turbojets, this fascinating variant was modified by General Dynamics through the installation of wings with a span

This WB-57F of the 7407th Combat Support Squadron, USAF, closely resembled the RB-57F variant, two of which were loaned to Pakistan and operated by No. 24 Squadron, PAF, from 1963 until 1965. While largely retaining the fuselage, fin and horizontal stabilisers of the original B-57 (and thus the British-made Canberra bomber), the aircraft has huge nacelles for two Pratt & Whitney TF33-P-11 turbofans, plus detachable pods for Pratt & Whitney J60-P-9 turbojets, and a wing-span of 122 feet (37m). (USAF)

of more than 122ft (37m) and other modifications – which made it capable of reaching operational altitudes of up to 80,000ft (24,000m). Moreover, it received high-gain phased array antennae in its wingtips, an extended radome, and a canister package developed by HRB-Singer known as 'System 365' (and capable of semi-automatic signal collection with 12 continuously scanning receivers, capable of fixed-frequency coverage of pre-selected frequencies) installed in the bomb bay.[7]

Furthermore, the CIA helped the Pakistanis to modify two of their B-57Bs into RB-57Bs equipped for ELINT-gathering operations. In legal terms, all four aircraft remained US possessions and were 'on loan' to the Pakistan Air Force (PAF), on condition that they would be used solely for the purpose of gathering intelligence on the PRC and the USSR. To call this condition 'unrealistic' would be an understatement: US intelligence must have known not only that the Pakistani leadership was obsessed with wrestling the control of the dispute Kashmir from India, but also that the country was dominated by the its omnipresent Inter-Service Intelligence (ISI). Unsurprisingly, the Pakistanis were quick to put their national interests above all else.

The history of the Pakistani RB-57 operations remains shrouded in secrecy until this very day, and thus it remains unknown if they ever undertook any operations inside Indian airspace prior to the 1965 Indo-Pakistan War. What is known is that this sub-variant was operated by No. 24 Squadron, PAF, and seems to have earned itself the nick-name 'Droopy' – probably because its huge wings tended to 'bend down' when the aircraft was parked on the ground.

Nevertheless, India was quick in searching for a solution to counter them – and in finding one. In 1963, New Delhi ordered, and – between January 1964 and October 1965 – received a total of five S-75 SAM-sites and 144 V-750 missiles. Many more derivatives – and even more missiles – were to follow at a later date. In service with the Indian Air Force (IAF), the system was introduced to service by several squadrons, organised into an air defence wing, and designated the Surface-to-Air Guided Weapon (SAGW): however, this designation was eventually abandoned in favour of SAM, which is to be used in the rest of this narrative for the sake of easier understanding.

As far as is known, both the Pakistani RB-57s and the Indian S-75s saw their first action during the Indo-Pakistani War of autumn 1965. Late at night on 10 October 1965, the RB-57F flown by Squadron Leader Rashid Mir and Flying Officer Sultan Malik passed over several front-line air bases of the IAF at an altitude of 65,000ft (19,812m). With the available Indian interceptors proving unable to reach the high-flying intruder, the jet continued its mission unmolested until reaching Ambala on its return leg. At that point in time, it entered the engagement range of one of the IAF's S-75 SAM-sites and was taken by surprise. Out of three V-750 missiles, one missed, one exploded above, and another below the RB-57F, spraying it with shrapnel. Although badly damaged – ground crews subsequently counted more than 170 hits – the aircraft limped back to the safety of Pakistani airspace. While approaching Peshawar AB, Mir realised that the nose gear would not deploy: nevertheless, he made a skilful emergency landing on the main undercarriage only, and the jet came to rest in the crash barrier at the end of the runway. Thanks to the dedication of the ground crews of No. 24 Squadron, and help from the personnel of the Pakistan International Airlines, the RB-57F was repaired and subsequently returned to the USA, together with the other example: it was not for the first, and not for the last, time that a military aircraft loaned to the PAF by the Americans would be misappropriated by the PAF. On the other side, while not constituting a physical 'kill', the IAF's success was overshadowed by its overall questionable performance in this conflict with Pakistan.

This was also the most that the Indian-operated S-75s ever managed to achieve. During the 1971 Indo-Pakistani War, they were launched on several occasions, but all related claims remain unconfirmed. Indeed, it seems that decoy balloons released by the Pakistanis were responsible for most of the related reporting: although the PAF has subsequently confirmed the loss of two B-57Bs and one B-57C to the Indian air defences (and one RB-57B destroyed on the ground in an air raid), none was ever mentioned in connection with any of the IAF's S-75s.

Certainly enough, the Soviet-made SAM-system continued soldiering-on in India for decades longer. Indeed, some of the units equipped with it were deployed along the border with Pakistan during several emergencies, however they saw no action ever again. All the Indian S-75s were phased out between 1987 and 1992, and the above-described damage to the PAF-operated RB-57F thus remains their sole verifiable achievement.

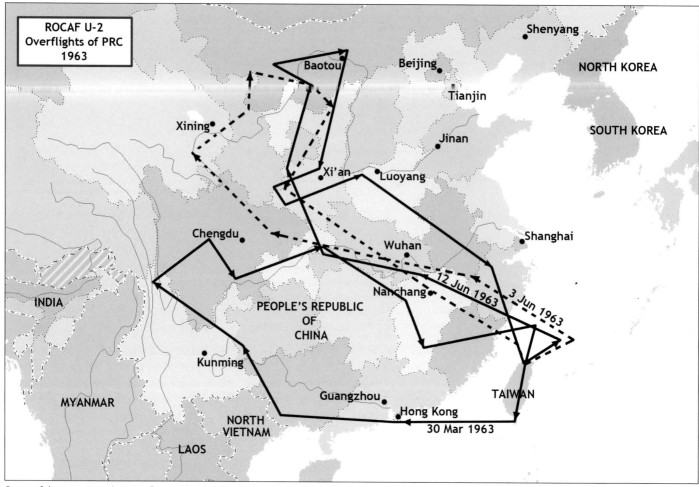

Some of the operational sorties flown over mainland China by the ROCAF's U-2s in 1963. (Map by Tom Cooper)

Red Flag

As previously mentioned, in 1957, the Soviets transferred to the PRC only enough equipment and missiles to equip four operational Sam-sites and one training SAM-site. Due to their own massive needs to protect major urban centres and military facilities, more was not possible at that point in time. Worse yet: while the Chinese would have been happy to acquire additional S-75s over the following years, political differences – foremost centred on the Beijing's refusal to accept its status as a 'junior partner' in relations with Moscow – came in between. Eventually, a deep disagreement between the USSR and the PRC developed, and the two communist regimes parted company. Amongst other issues, this resulted in all the Soviet military assistance and aid for China being virtually cut off. Obviously, this meant that the PLA could not expect to receive any further S-75 systems, nor even any kind of replacement missiles. Left without a choice, the Chinese launched work on 'cloning' the entire S-75 system.

Initial work was launched in August 1961, when the Bureau of Machinery and Electronics No.2 was set-up in Shanghai to manage the program designated the Hong Qi-1 (Red Flag 1, or HQ-1). The work on cloning the missiles proceeded at high pace, and just two years later, in June 1963, the first test-flight of the resulting HQ-1 missile was undertaken. Subsequently, the Chinese went on to progressively upgrade the original by improving their propulsion and electronics. Moreover, in order to improve the mobility of the entire system, they installed missile launchers on a derivative of the chassis for the Type 63 light tank. The result was the HQ-2. However, just when the entire project gained traction, the Cultural Revolution struck. In 1966 purges of leading engineers and much of the involved workforce almost destroyed the country's aerospace industry and massively slowed

down the pace of further progress. The work on a copy of the RSNA-75 radar experienced severe problems and for most of the 1960s the Chinese never managed to manufacture more than three or four of them. Indeed, the first HQ-2s entered operational service only in July 1967, and it was only in the early 1970s that the mass production of the system began.

Nevertheless, the availability of the few HQ-1s and additional equipment gradually enabled the PLA to increase the number of operational units and thus provide SAM-protection for ever more locations. In turn, this made the overflights by the ROCAF U-2s ever riskier. The results were not long in the waiting.

The final U-2 loss to SAMs

As so often between 1960 and 1965, the January 1965 shoot-down of the 35th Black Cat Squadron's U-2 over China resulted in yet another temporary and rather short halt of the joint CIA-Taiwanese operations. Indeed, the next overflight was launched in February of the same year and was quickly followed by two more. The reason was the US concern about the progress of the Chinese nuclear program, and especially the related testing. Correspondingly, the Taiwanese U-2s became highly active, and flew no fewer than 30 reconnaissance sorties over the PRC by the end of the year. Of course, the expression 'highly active' was relative: while nothing special for other types of aircraft, it should be kept in mind that every U-2 mission was a very special, extensively planned and prepared event. Subsequently, the number of overflights decreased: only 10 were flown in 1966, although the PRC conducted its – meanwhile – third test of a nuclear bomb. Even the 'surge' in 1967 remained minimal: 14 missions were flown.

By this time the CIA had initiated Project Tabasco, which aimed

Fin of Chang Li-yi's U-2C 'Article 358' (3512), shot down over the PRC on 10 January 1965. Notable is the application of the Taiwanese national insignia on the rear fuselage (for further details, see the colour section). (via Tom Cooper)

Another view of the 3512's wreck. (via Tom Cooper)

The first commander ever to deploy the S-75 SAM-system in combat against an aircraft, and also the most successful 'U-2 Hunter' ever: Yue Zhenhua, commander of the 2nd Surface-to-Air Guided Missile Battalion of the PLA, the unit that shot down four high-flying Taiwanese aircraft, including three U-2s between 1962 and 1964. This photograph shows him during a reception by Chairman Mao Tse Tung. (via Tom Cooper)

to develop a sensor pod that could be dropped into the Taklamakan Desert near the Lop Nor nuclear test site. The pod was intended to deploy an antenna after landing and transmit the collected data to the US SIGINT station at Shiulinkou on Taiwan. After nearly a year of development and testing, the pod was prepared and two pilots of the 35th Black Cat Squadron trained to deploy it. On 7 May 1967, the U-2 'Article 383' piloted by Spike Chuang launched from Takhli Royal Thai Air Force Base, with one such pod under each wing. Although successfully releasing them near the Lop Nur nuclear weapons test base, no data was ever recovered from either – much to chagrin of the CIA. The PRC tested its first thermonuclear device on 17 June 1967. In an attempt to remedy the situation, on 31 August 1967, Bill Chang flew another sortie into this area, but without success and again nothing was heard from the pods.[8]

Meanwhile, despite the Cultural Revolution, the PLA was working hard on improving its air defence capabilities, and one of the first operational HQ-2 SAM-systems was pressed into service with the newly established 14th Surface-to-Air Guided Missile Battalion. On 8 September 1967, this unit – commanded by Xia Cunfeng – ambushed the U-2A 'Article 373' flown by Huang Jung-Bei (Tom Huang) underway over Zehijang, and promptly shot it down. Tragically, the incident proved fatal for the pilot.

With hindsight, it is possible to say that this was the last successful hunt for a U-2 – not only over China, but ever. Certainly enough, the PRC was to claim additional high-flying jets of the ROCAF as shot down on 2 April 1968, in January 1969, on 16 May 1969, and in 1970. However, in 1968, the few remaining U-2C/F/Gs of the 35th Black Cat Squadron were replaced by the newer U-2Rs (the first mission

flown by the new type took place on 8 April 1969). As far as is known, they flew only two flights into the PRC's airspace: on the contrary, all further incursions were discontinued. Instead, starting in 1969, the Taiwanese U-2s only flew peripheral missions, always carefully remaining outside Chinese airspace while collecting intelligence with the help of oblique photography, or through ELINT and SIGINT-gathering. Even then, these missions were not without hazards – because now it was the interceptors of the PLAAF and the PLANAF which attempted to intercept them.

Interceptor Problems

The story of the hunt for the U-2 would be incomplete without taking at least a brief look at attempts by manned Chinese interceptors to catch one of the high-flying intruders. The PLAAF and the PLANAF had essentially sealed the sky against low-flying ROCAF aircraft underway over mainland China just by using their first-generation jets, like the MiG-15s and MiG-17s, in the late 1950s and early 1960s. However, high-flying reconnaissance aircraft remained outside their reach. The situation did not improve even once Moscow – on request from Beijing – granted the licence for the domestic manufacture of the MiG-19P, and provided the necessary technical documentation, in October 1957. Although the PRC subsequently launched series production of three variants of these, and greatly improved the overall reliability of the original design, the break with the USSR and the subsequent Cultural Revolution resulted in a mass of problems that greatly slowed down their service entry. Correspondingly, the PLAAF and the PLANAF still had next to no MiG-19s in operational service through the early 1960s. Almost the same was valid for the Chinese efforts to obtain the next – and then particularly important – Soviet interceptor-design, and then one that was, at least theoretically capable of reaching the U-2's operational altitudes: the MiG-21F-13s.[9]

The contract for the technology-transfer of the MiG-21F-13 and its Tumansky R-11F-300 engine to China was signed on 30 March 1962 during the short improvement in relations between Beijing and Moscow. It resulted in the delivery of about two dozen jets in the form of knock-down kits for assembly in China. However, before the Soviets were able to transfer all of the technical documentation necessary for their manufacture, relations between Beijing and Moscow cooled again. The subsequent Cultural Revolution almost drove a nail into the coffin of the entire project: whatever engineers were left to work had to resort to reverse engineering of many crucial parts. The available MiG-21F-13s were assembled and pressed into service with the PLAAF, while a few were kept back to be used as specimens for further research and development of their indigenous variant, the J-7.[10]

Thou shall ... and thou shall not

Even then, this was only the beginning of the true problems – nearly all of which were related to the construction of this 'light-weight, point-defence interceptor'. Certainly enough, the tactical manual for deployment of the MiG-21F-13 against high-flying targets was envisaging operations up to an altitude of 80,000ft (24,384m), but actually getting there, finding, intercepting, aiming at and hitting a target – were all entirely different pairs of shoes. The first problem was the jet's short range: no matter what version, the MiG-21 was always short on fuel, and even the tactical manual advised the pilot to constantly keep an eye on the fuel gauge. The Chinese solved the problem by scrambling their MiG-21s relatively early, and first bringing them to a patrol station at an altitude of 7,000-8,500 metres (22,966-27,887ft), somewhere across the predicted route of the incoming U-2 – before initiating the actual intercept.

A close-up photograph of the Chinese-manufactured HQ-1 or HQ-2: both included diverse improvements in comparison to the original V-750/11D missile. (via Tom Cooper)

Another problem was the aircraft's construction: the MiG-21F-13 had a thick, armoured Plexiglas windshield, which heavily restricted visibility straight ahead. This issue was massive enough to be considered even in the tactical manual for this variant, which instructed:

An important peculiarity of the MiG-21F-13 is the substantial reduction (by approximately 1-1.5 times) in target detection range when looking through the armoured plexiglass…The range for detecting a single fighter when looking through the side canopy is approximately 5km (3 miles); however, when looking through the bullet-proof glass of the front windscreen, the range is reduced to 2 or 3km (1.2-1.8 miles). Therefore, visual search should be conducted through the side canopy…In consideration of this, it is advisable that the interceptor be vectored so that the target detection will take place basically through the unarmoured portion of the side glass.[11]

The U-2 was – for all practical purposes – a 'fighter-sized' target except when seen from below or (rarely) above, but especially as seen from the rear, which was the classic attack route for the majority of contemporary interceptors. Unsurprisingly, the same manual advised MiG-21 pilots that:

When intercepting at an altitude about 46,000-49,000ft (14,021-14,935m), or higher, then necessity of vectoring at any angle off the tail other than zero requires the guidance of the interceptor at an altitude lower than the target in order to increase its manoeuvring

during vectoring.[12]

In other words: the ground control was supposed to bring the MiG-21 into a position below and to the side of the U-2 before the actual attack, so that the pilot could first acquire the target visually. Otherwise, a successful interception was unlikely. From there, the pilot was supposed to manoeuvre and bring his weapons to bear, all the time flying in the thin atmosphere and on the verge of the fighter's envelope. The final issue was that of the approach speed, with regards to which the tactical manual warned of an approach at much too high a closure rate: essentially, even if brought into a perfect attack position, the MiG-21 pilot had only a handful of seconds to visually acquire the target, establish a lock-on with his air-to-air missiles, and fire.

A Matter of Arts – and Luck

Mastering all of this, meant that a successful interception was an act of the highest piloting skill – and a truckload of luck: during the final moments of intercepting a U-2, the MiG-21F-13 was effectively out of control, underway along a ballistic trajectory, with minimal to no opportunity to acquire the target and open fire. It is unsurprising that at least one US U-2 pilot underway over Cuba in the late 1960s experienced a rude shock when a MiG-21 actually shot over the top of his aircraft before tumbling out of control into the thicker air down below. Still, the new threat was taken seriously enough for the Taiwanese to equip their U-2s with the same Sugar Scoop exhaust cover already introduced to service on USAF U-2s: this was an 18-inch extension of the lower portion of the engine exhaust, applied to

Proud of achievements of its SAM-operators, Beijing eventually put on display the wreckage of all four U-2s shot down by its S-75 units. (Albert Grandolini Collection)

shield the hottest part of the aircraft from infra-red guided air-to-air missiles – such as the R-3S, the principal weapon of the MiG-21F-13.

From what is known, the first successful interception attempt by PLAAF MiG-21F-13s appears to have been staged only on 14 March 1965, when Lieutenant Wu Zaixi (Wu Tsai-hsi) of the 35th Black Cat Squadron reported seeing smoke plumes like those from air-to-air missiles passing by his aircraft. Whether this was the case remains a mystery, but Wu's aircraft was not damaged and he returned safely. Another, similar incident followed on 27 May 1965, when the cameras of the U-2 piloted by Wang Sijue (Wang His-chüeh) actually photographed a Chinese MiG-21F-13 passing below it, almost close enough to touch, yet still too far away to successfully engage.

Additional intercept attempts certainly followed, and indeed Beijing seems to have claimed Taiwanese U-2s as shot down on 2 April 1968, in January 1969, on 16 May 1969, and in 1970, although none was actually lost at these dates. What is certain is that on 29 April 1971, the U-2R flown by Lieutenant-Colonel Shen Zongli (Shen Thung-li) was underway at an altitude of 22,265m (73,047ft) into a reconnaissance of Dalian and Lüshun on the Lianoning Peninsula, when his RWR and the System 20 – a rear-hemisphere infra-red warning device – warned him of a threat

from left aft. The pilot made a slight turn to the left, and the warning disappeared. However, a few seconds later there was a new warning, this time about a threat from the right after side. It was only at this point in time the that Taiwanese pilot was able to see a MiG-21F-13 alongside his wing – at least for two seconds: the interceptor then dropped down and out of sight.

Ultimately, neither the PLAAF nor the PLANAF ever managed to shoot down any ROCAF U-2s with their manned interceptors. While occasionally capable of reaching the altitude at which the reconnaissance jets were operating, and sometimes getting quite close, even the MiG-21 proved unable to maintain position for long enough to engage successfully. Thus, the efforts by the Chinese pilots were

This dramatic photograph was taken by reconnaissance cameras of Wang Sijue's U-2 on 27 May 1965, and shows a PLAAF MiG-21 flashing by his aircraft, too close for comfort! (ROCAF, via Albert Grandolini)

A diagram reconstructing the incident of 29 April 1971, perhaps the day on which a MiG-21 came closest to actually intercepting a U-2. Notable is that the MiG-21 could not change its course during this encounter, while the U-2 – thanks to its huge wing – managed to 'outmanoeuvre' the smaller interceptor. (Diagram by Tom Cooper)

never rewarded with an actual 'kill'.

Sad Part of the Story

While the MiG-21s thus remained unsuccessful, many other dangers related to flying operations at very high altitudes threatened the lives of the U-2 pilots. Perhaps the most dramatic demonstration of this fact was on 16 May 1969, when the aircraft flown by Lieutenant Zhang Xie (Chang Hsieh), disappeared without a trace over the Yellow Sea. He is presumed to have crashed due to a malfunction of the controls – and was never found, despite a week-long intensive search. The 35th Black Cat Squadron of the ROCAF continued its operations into the early 1970s, though with a much-reduced tempo. One of the reasons were restrictions placed upon their operations due to US President Richard Nixon's official visit to Beijing in 1972. Indeed, the unit flew its last known operational sortie only two years later, on 11 April 1974, after which the surviving U-2Rs were returned to the USA.

While the Taiwanese overflights thus ended for all practical purposes, the human side of their effort should not be ignored – alone because of the particularly sad fate of the two captured pilots, who,

French Attempts

Whoever might think that the U-2 was deployed to fly reconnaissance missions over the USSR, the PRC or their allies only, is deadly wrong. Indeed, the jet is known to have seen 'action' over several 'allied' nations, just like its predecessor, the RB-57. In July 1963, a pair of the then brand-new Dassault Mirage IIICJ interceptors is known to have intercepted an RB-57A of the USAF and forced it to land at Lod International Airport, in Israel. The high-flying reconnaissance aircraft was underway from Saudi Arabia to Turkey and involved in monitoring the construction of the Israeli nuclear complex in Dimona.[14]

In June 1967 – a year after French President Charles de Gaulle withdrew his country from NATO – early warning radars of the French Air Force detected a U-2 underway in the direction of one of the country's nuclear facilities. A Mirage IIIE of the 2nd Fighter Wing (2ème Escadre de Chasse) was promptly scrambled from Dijon Air Base, with the task of intercepting the intruder. Equipped with the SEPR 841 rocket booster, the interceptor literally soared into the skies, though not with the aim of actually shooting down the US aircraft – but to photograph it: photographs were of crucial importance for enabling Paris to provide evidence for a violation of its airspace in the case of the US denial. After climbing to an altitude of 45,000ft (13,716m), the French pilot engaged his SEPR booster, which accelerated his Mirage to Mach 1.8, and enabled it to reach an altitude of 65,000ft (19,812m). While slightly decelerating to Mach 1.7, the French pilot caught with the U-2 as this was underway at Mach 0.9 and almost directly above Dijon AB. Although wearing the bulky and uncomfortable high-altitude suit, he managed to take a photograph with an 'average civilian camera', before nearly colliding with his 'target' while keeping it centred in his camera's optical visor. Critically short on fuel after such a high-speed climb, the Mirage pilot then switched off the booster and glided back to base. While it is certain that the US pilot was warned about being intercepted, because all of the U-2s were equipped with advanced ECM-systems, it flew no evasion manoeuvres. French sources think that the U-2 pilot was quite shocked by what happened next – first by the supersonic shock wave of the French interceptor, and then the Mirage flashing by underneath his nose. What is certain is that the USA subsequently stopped all overflights of France and would not return until years later – and then with Mach 3-capable Lockheed SR-71As at an altitude of 75,000ft (22,860m)![15]

A U-2R of the 35th Black Cat Squadron, ROCAF. Notable is the application of only a very small national insignia on the rear fuselage, and a four-digit serial on the fin. The 19 U-2C/Fs and U-2Rs loaned to the ROCAF by the CIA flew a total of 220 operational missions. (Albert Grandolini Collection)

despite surviving their shoot-downs experienced a 'hard landing'. Yeh Chang-di and Chang Li-yi remained in the custody of the PRC: the authorities considered declaring them as 'prisoners of war' to be 'unfitting', because Beijing considered the Taiwanese as Chinese too. While not being subjected to brutal and elaborate torture, they were kept in solitary confinement for years, and then assigned to village communes where hard physical work and meagre food were the norm. Moreover, Beijing never officially announced that they were still alive and thus their whereabouts remained unknown to Taiwan, eventually prompting the local authorities to declare them as deceased, 'in absentia'. Rather unsurprisingly, both of their wives – now officially widows – remarried. Worst of all, when they were finally released, on 10 November 1982, via Hong Kong – back then still under the British jurisdiction – they experienced nothing short of a major disgrace: the Taiwanese government refused their entry. Fortunately, they were helped by retired US and Taiwanese pilots, even by the CIA, and permitted to settle down in the USA. Rather ironically, a foreign intelligence agency that often mistreated even its US employees, proved more caring towards the Taiwanese pilots than their own government.[13]

9
LAST BLAST

The definite end of Taiwanese U-2 operations – or, arguably, the early termination of direct overflights of mainland China by the ROCAF – ended an important chapter in the confrontation of the two, and then three, superpowers, the USA, USSR and the PRC. Symbolically, it ended the maturing period in relations between these nations, dominated by fierce rivalry. Of course, it was not the end of the story about the hunt for the U-2, or the further development and upgrades of the aircraft itself, or the countermeasures against it that all experienced massive improvements over the following years. Indeed, the deployment of the S-75 SAM-system taught everybody involved a mass of crucial lessons about electronic warfare: from just a handful of encounters the US intelligence and military services learned about the system's susceptibility to electronic countermeasures and the lack of tactical mobility. Meanwhile, the U-2 underwent a major redesign, gained bigger wings and an enlarged fuselage: covering these stories would be well outside the scope of this volume. Having said that, at the very least it is possible to present a relatively recent example of confrontation between these old adversaries and, in case of the missiles, perhaps their final combat use.

The Final Confrontation
The events described above do not cover all U-2 operations during the Cold War, nor those by this type during the Vietnam War, for this was never the purpose of this volume. The said operations have been described with much detail in a number of publications including those composed of declassified CIA files. Moreover, the actual topic of this volume has been the attempts to intercept the type and its closest predecessors – whether by manned interceptors or SAMs. This volume would be incomplete without mentioning at least two additional attempts to 'hunt a U-2' – both of which took place relatively recently.

On 25 March 1995, a MiG-25 interceptor of the Iraqi Air Force was scrambled and vectored to intercept a U-2 of the US Air Force underway over Iraq. However, the Iraqi pilot was forced to disengage when approached by two McDonnell-Douglas F-15C Eagle interceptors of the USAF.[1]

It was also in Iraqi skies that the U-2 met its old foe the S-75 SAM-system for the last time. The Iraqis were attempting to shoot-down American and other Western aircraft for years during the 1990s, but with the exception of a few UAVs were by large unsuccessful. One reason for this being that virtually any emission of SAM guidance

Table 4: Successful RB-57 and U-2 Hunters[4]				
Date	Weapon	Pilot/SAM-site CO	Unit	Vanquished & Notes
18 Feb 1958	MiG-17F (?)	unknown	unknown, PLAAF or PLANAF	ROCAF RB-57A 52-1431 (ROCAF serial 5642), hit over Shandong, pilot Guang-Huia Chao killed
7 Oct 1959	S-75 (SA-2)	Yue Zhenhua	2nd Surface-to-Air Guided Missile Battalion, PLA	ROCAF RB-57D 53-3978 (ROCAF serial 5643), hit over Beijing, pilot Ying Chin Wong killed
1 May 1960	S-75 (SA-2)	Mikhail Voronov	2nd Battalion, 57th Anti-Aircraft Missile Brigade, PVO	CIA U-2A Article 360, hit over Sverdlovsk, pilot Francis G Powers, ejected and captured
9 Sep 1962	S-75 (SA-2)	Yue Zhenhua	2nd Surface-to-Air Guided Missile Battalion, PLA	ROCAF U-2C Article 378 (ROCAF serial 352), hit over Nanchang, Major Huai Chen ejected but died of injuries
27 Oct 1962	S-75 (SA-2)	Ivan Gerchenkov	1st Battalion, 507th Air Defence Regiment, V-PVO	USAF U-2F 56-6676, hit over Cuba, pilot Rudolf Anderson killed
1 Nov 1963	S-75 (SA-2)	Yue Zhenhua	2nd Surface-to-Air Guided Missile Battalion, PLA	ROCAF U-2 Article 355 (ROCAF serial 3511), hit over Jaingxi, Major Yeh Changti/Robin Yeh ejected and captured
7 July 1964	S-75 (SA-2)	Yue Zhenhua	2nd Surface-to-Air Guided Missile Battalion, PLA	ROCAF U-2G Article 362 (no serial or ROCAF roundels applied), hit over Jiangxi, Lieutenant-Colonel Lee Nanpin/Terry Lee killed
10 Jan 1965	S-75 (SA-2)	unknown	1st Surface-to-Air Guided Missile Battalion, PLA	ROCAF U-2C Article 358 (USAF FY-serial 56-6691, ROCAF serial 3512), hit over Baotou, inner Mongolia, Major Chang Li-yi/Jack Chang ejected and captured
10 Oct 1965	S-75 (SA-2)	unknown	unknown, IAF	PAF RB-57F hit and damaged over Ambala, western India, crew made a successful emergency landing
8 Sep 1967	HQ-2 (CSA-2)	Xia Cunfeng	14th Surface-to-Air Guided Missile Battalion, PLAAF	ROCAF U-2A Article 373 (no serial applied; possibly no ROCAF roundels either), hit over Jiangsu, Captain Huang Jung-Bei killed

radars illuminating Western aircraft was sure to result in a retaliatory attack by anti-radar missiles or other weapons. A possible solution to avoid this was to fire SAMs on a ballistic trajectory without employing electronic guidance. For this to have any chance of achieving a hit, the target had to fly along a predictable course, all the time maintaining constant speed and altitude. This is exactly how the U-2s operated and it was an aircraft of this type which was engaged by the Iraqis on 25 July 2001. The missile launched at the U-2 exploded well behind and below that reconnaissance aircraft as this was underway over southern Iraq at an altitude of more than 21,000m (over 70,000ft). The jet suffered no damage, but the pilot later reported feeling the shock of the missile's detonation, which indicates this was a 'close call', indeed.[2]

This is likely to remain the last time any U-2 would be threatened in this fashion, if for no other reason than because the S-75 has meanwhile been withdrawn from service all around the world. On the other hand, the considerably modified variants of the U-2 continue soldiering on with the USAF.

Old Soldiers do not fade away: they go out with a Bang

The S-75 family of surface-to-air missiles is seeing the twilight of its career, for over time it became increasingly obsolete. Many of the armed forces equipped with these SAM systems have decommissioned them and in not a few cases they were either destroyed in combat or fell into disrepair as the nations operating them have descended into chaos.

As an exception, one of the few countries retaining the S-75/SA-2 in any significant numbers was Yemen. The said nation had a turbulent history going through partition, unification and civil war. In the years 2014 – 15 the faction gaining the upper hand in Yemen's internal struggle was the Houthi (Ansar Allah) movement which de-facto sized power in the north of country. This in turn provoked a military intervention led by Saudi Arabia and backed by the West. Among their first actions the Saudis struck Yemeni surface-to-surface and surface-to-air missile sites, as well as storage facilities, eliminating early on a large part of their adversary's offensive and defensive missile capabilities. Having the benefit of support from US intelligence and many informers on the ground, the Saudis knew where to strike in order to achieve the desired effect. The few SAM sites which survived the initial onslaught were knocked out with relative ease by means of stand-off weapons. In turn, the S-75 failed to achieve any 'kills', bar the possible shooting-down of a UAV. While this SAM system proved to be ineffective as an air defence weapon when used against an aerial opponent possessing modern weapons and electronic warfare capabilities it, or more precisely its missiles, could still be used with a measure of success in the surface-to-surface role. Appropriately modified and fired on a ballistic trajectory they have a fairly decent chance to hit their intended targets on the ground. Thus, the S-75/SA-2 may not fade away but literally go out with a bang.[3]

BIBLIOGRAPHY

Allen, K., Krumel, G. & Pollack, J. D., *China's Air Force Enters the 21st Century* (Santa Monica: RAND, 1995) (ISBN 0-8330-1648-2)

Bergin, B., 'The Growth of China's Air Defenses: Responding to Covert Overflights, 1949–1974', *Studies in Intelligence*, Vol. 57, No. 2, June 2013

Bromley, L. R., *Flight of the Dragon: A Taiwanese U-2 Pilot's Long Journey to Freedom* (Solihull: Helion & Co., 2017) (ISBN 9781911096481)

Chen, F. F., 'Double Ten Mazu Air Combat', 'Nine Eight Cheng Hai Air Combat', 'Eight Fourteen Ping-Tan Air Combat', 'Red Santa' and others (translations of official PLAAF and ROCAF reports about air combats during the [Third] Taiwan Strait Crisis, 1958, and operations by the PLA's SA-2 units to intercept ROCAF RB-57s and U-2s, provided in 2001)

CHOU, Y., *Return of the Sabre* (Taipei: Wen Ching Wen Ku, 1995)

CIA, 'U-2 Inventory', *Memorandum IDEA-2805-65*, 26 October 1965 (CIA, FOIA Electronic Reading Room)

CIA, 'U-2 Procurement and Losses', *Memorandum IDEA-3239-66*, 12 July 1966 (CIA, FOIA Electronic Reading Room)

CIA, 'U-2 Procurement and Losses', *Memorandum IDEA-0581-67*, 25 October 1967 (CIA, FOIA Electronic Reading Room)

Demin, A., *Aviation of the Big Neighbour, Volume 2* (Moscow: Fond Sodeystviya Aviatsiy, 2012) (ISBN: 978-5-903389-55-1) (in Russian)

Dokuchayev, A., 'Okhota v stratosfere', *Aviatsiya i Kosmonavtika* magazine, Vol. 4/2000

Dobbs, M., *One Minute to Midnight: Kennedy, Khrushchev and Castro on the Brink of Nuclear War* (London: Hutchinson Radius, 2008) (ISBN: 0091796660)

Fensch, T., *The C.I.A. and the U-2 Program 1954–1974* (New Century Books, 2001) (ISBN: 0-930751-09-4)

Flintham, V., *Air Wars and Aircraft: A Detailed Record of Air Combat 1945 to the Present* (London: Arms and Armour Press, 1989) (ISBN 0-85368-779-X)

Fowler, M.J.F., 'The Application of Declassified KH-7 GAMBIT Satellite Photographs to Studies of Cold War Material culture: A Case Study from the Former Soviet Union', *Antiquity* No. 82(317), September 2008

Fu, J. K., *Secret of the Pass* (Taipei: Wings of China, 1992) (in Chinese)

Grimes, Col. W. (USAF, ret.), *The History of Big Safari* (Bloomington: Archway Publishing, 2014) (ISBN: 978-1-4808-0456-2)

Hua, M. H., 'The Black Cat Squadron', *Air Power History*, Spring 2002 (in Chinese)

Hua, M. H., *Sky of Military Aircraft: From Thunderjet to U-2* (Taipei: Commonwealth Publishing Co. 1999) (in Chinese)

Hua, M. H., *The Lost Black Cats: Story of the Two Captured Chinese U-2 Pilots* (Author House, 2005)

Jackson, R., *High Cold War: Strategic Air Reconnaissance and the Electronic Intelligence War* (Sparkford: Patrick Stephens Ltd./ Haynes Publishing, 1998) (ISBN: 1-85260-584-7)

Jenkins, D. R., *Lockheed U-2 Dragon Lady; Warbird Tech Vol 16* (Specialty Press Publishers and Wholesalers, 1998) (ISBN: 1-58007-009-4)

Lai, B., *The Dragon's Teeth: The Chinese People's Liberation Army, Its History, Traditions, and Air and Sea Capability in the 21st Century* (Oxford: Casemate, 2016) (ISBN 9781612003894)

Miller, J., *Lockheed U-2* (Aerofax Inc, 1983) (ISBN: 0-942548-04-3)

Nimitz, Ch. W., *Sea Power: A Naval History* (Müchen, 1982) (in German)

Pedlow, G. W. & Welzenbach, D. E., *The Central Intelligence Agency and Overhead Reconnaissance: The U-2 and OXCART Programs, 1954-1974* (Washington DC, Central Intelligence Agency, History Staff, 1992)

Pocock, C., *50 Years of the U-2: The Complete Illustrated History of the Dragon Lady* (Atglen: Schiffer Publishing Ltd., 2004) (ISBN: 978-0764323461)

Pocock, C. *Dragon Lady: The History of the U-2 Spyplane* (Osceola: Motorbooks International, 1989)

Pocock, C., *The Black Bats: CIA Spy Flights over China from Taiwan, 1951-1969* (Atglen: Schiffer Military History, 2010) (ISBN: 978-0-7643-3513-6)

Potter, S. B., Nimitz, C. W., Rohwer, J., *Sea Power: A Naval History*, (Englewood Cliffs: Prentice-Hall Inc., 1982) (ISBN: 3-88199-082-8)

Powers, F. G., with Gentry C., *Operation Overflight: The U-2 spy pilot tells his story for the first time* (New York: Holt, Rinehart and Winston, 1970) (ISBN: 03-083045-1)

Richardson, D., *Techniques and Equipment of Electronic Warfare* (London: Salamander Books Ltd., 1985) (ISBN: 0-86101-265-8)

Rivas, S., *Playa Girón: The Cuban Exiles' Invasion at the Bay of Pigs, 1961* (Solihull: Helion & Co., 2014)

Thompson, Sir R. (consulting editor), *War in Peace: An Analysis of Warfare since 1945*, (London: Orbis Publishing, 1981) (ISBN: 0-85613-341-8)

Tufail, K., *Against all Odds: The Pakistan Air Force in the 1971 India-Pakistan War* (Warwick: Helion & Co., 2020)

Wen-Shiao, L., *Chinese Air Force in Action, Vol.2* (publisher unclear, 1991) (in Chinese)

White, W. L, *The Little Toy Dog; the story of the two RB-47 flyers, Captain John R. McKone and Captain Freeman B. Olmstead* (New York: Dutton 1962) (ISBN: 0525147594)

Whitten, Col. H. W., Blyden, E. & Pocock, C., *Without a Warning: The Avoidable Shootdown of a U-2 Spyplane During the Cuban Missile Crisis* (CreateSpace Independent Publishing Platform, 2018) (ISBN: 978-1986237642)

Wong, T.S. & Pocock, C., *Blackcats Squadron: The Story of U-2* (Taipei: Lien-Ching, 1990) (in Chinese)

Zaloga, S., *Red SAM: The SA-2 Guideline Anti-Aircraft Missile* (Oxford: Osprey Publishing Ltd, 2007) (ISBN 978-1-84603-062-8)

Zolotarev, Major-General V. A., *Russia (USSR) in Local Wars and Regional Conflicts in the Second Half of the 20th Century* (Moscow: 2000) (in Russian)

Online Sources

Air Combat Information Group (ACIG), forum and database at acig.info

Delalande, A., 'Warning – MiG-25!', *warisboring.com*

Gupta A. & Pillarisetti J., 'The S-75 Dvina – India's first Surface-to-Air Guided Weapon', bharat-rakshak.com/

Hua, Gen. H. M., http://roadrunnersinternationale.com/hua.html

Isaev, S., *Pages of the History of the 32nd Guards Fighter Aviation Regiment: Part 1, The 32nd Guards Fighter Aviation Regiment in Cuba, 1962-1963* (in Russian), (online publication available at militera.lib.ru and/or airforce.ru)

Isaev, S., *Pages of the History of the 32*nd *Guards Fighter Aviation Regiment: Part 2, Shatalovo, 1968-1989* (in Russian) (online publication available at militera.lib.ru and/or airforce.ru)

Newlin, G., 'The Case of the Runaway U-2', *airspacemag.com*

NSA, 'Interview with Grigory Romanovich Danilevich, Colonel, Head of the Political Section of the PVO Division', nsarchive2.gwu.edu

Pamyatnik, 'Raketa V-300 zenitno raketnaya systema S-25 Berkut, Izdeliye 217m, zav No.6222618/6222655', *c-25.su*

Raspletin, Dr. A. A., 'History PVO', historykpvo.narod2.ru

Unknown, *Eastern Order of Battle*, easternorbat.com

Unknown, 'Illustrated Guide to Moscow Anti-Aircraft Defense System', *allworldwars.com*

Unknown, 'The Lost Black Cats', *zonaeuropa.com*

Unknown, 'The Blackcat Squadron U-2 Operation', *taiwanairpower. org*

VFP-62 OPERATIONS OVER CUBA, 'The Cuban Missile Crisis', *vfp62.com*

Zaloga, S., 'Defending the Kremlin: The First Generation of Soviet Strategic Air Defense Systems 1950-60' *bobrowen.com*

NOTES

Foreword

1 Unless stated otherwise, this chapter is based upon Pedlow et al *The Central Intelligence Agency and Overhead reconnaissance: The U-2 and OXCART Programs.*

Chapter 1

1 Unless stated otherwise, this sub-chapter is based upon Zaloga, *Red SAM.*

2 Pamyatnik, *Raketa V-300.* Notably, testing of the S-25 ran from 2 November 1952. Testing against Tu-4 drones ran from 26 April until 18 May 1953, by when a total of 81 test-firings had been undertaken. Additional tests were done in September and October 1953, and the first full-scale operational S-25 system was built at Kapustin Yar in January 1954. By 1 April 1955, another series of tests ran including 69 launches at Ilyushin Il-28 and Tu-4 drones (including a simultaneous launch of 20 missiles against 20 targets. For further details, see Fowler, pp. 717-719.

3 Only the sites deployed permanently to garrison specific sections of airspace enjoyed the benefit of concrete structures and hard surface roads.

4 Raspletin, *historykpvo.narod2.ru.* Notably, the initial production rate fell well behind plan. For example, in 1957, the Soviets planned to manufacture a total of 40 S-75 sites, and 1,200 missiles, but managed only 30 and 621, respectively.

5 Unless stated otherwise, this chapter is based upon Pedlow et al.

Chapter 2

1 Dokuchayev, 'Okhota v Stratosfere'.

Chapter 3

1 Unless stated otherwise, this chapter is based upon Demin, *Aviation of the Big Neighbour.*

2 The RB-57A (ROCAF serial 5642, US FY serial 52-1431, piloted by Guang-Huia Chao, who was killed) was one of ten such aircraft modified for the US Air Force as part of Project Heart Throb for overflights of the Soviet Far East. Two of them were provided to Taiwan in September 1957 for operations over the PRC. Sources differ over exactly what kind of interceptors achieved this feat, some citing MiG-15bis, others MiG-17Fs, and yet others Chinese-manufactured J-5As – a MiG-17F manufactured under licence in China. Considering the operational altitude of such aircraft as the RB-57A, the version of the story with the MiG-17F is the most likely one: the type was brand-new in the PLAAF's service as of early 1958.

3 Raspletin, Table 'SAM Exports', *historykpvo.narod2.ru*

4 Once Slusar's tenure in the PRC was over he returned to the USSR.

Subsequently, he served in the V-PVO, eventually attaining the rank of a Major-General, and then settling in Belarus on his retirement. Once this former Soviet republic gained independence, he was invited to the Chinese embassy in Minsk as an honorary guest in recognition for his achievements from decades earlier.

Chapter 4

1 Unless stated otherwise, this chapter is based upon Pedlow et al.

2 Dokuchaev, 'Okhota v Stratosphere'.

Chapter 5

1 Unless stated otherwise, this chapter is based upon Pedlow et al.

2 The description of Soviet efforts to bring down Powers' U-2 in this and the following sub-chapters is based upon Dokuchayev, 'Okhota v Stratosfere'.

3 The time is often quoted as 08:53, but this appears to be the time when Major Voronov reported the target's destruction and not when it was actually engaged.

4 This small amount of explosives could not have destroyed the whole aircraft: the charge was placed so as to obliterate the photographic equipment.

5 Presently the wreckage is exhibited at the Central Armed Forces Museum in Moscow with a number of small fragments donated to a few other museums. In the latter context it is interesting to note, that once the USSR had been dissolved, Russia handed over some small fragments of the aircraft to the United States which can be seen at the National Cryptologic Museum in Fort George G. Meade, Maryland.

6 Safronov's death was officially acknowledged only in the late 1980s and early 1990s.

Chapter 6

1 Unless stated otherwise, this chapter is based upon Powers & Gentry, *Operation Overflight.*

2 White, *The Little Toy Dog.*

3 The events described above in a rather brief fashion were related in detail by White in his book *Little Toy Dog* – titled after a small toy dog mascot which major Palm carried with him for luck.

Chapter 7

1 Ibid; Flintham, pp. 347-349 & Rivas, pp. 9-21.

2 Isaev, *Pages of the History of the 32*nd *Guards Fighter Regiment* & NSA, 'Interview with Grigory Romanovich Danilevich'.

3 The 32nd GIAP was re-established once its personnel returned from Cuba.

4 Ironically, one of the USAF's RF-101 pilots involved in these operations was Captain Carl Overstreet – the same pilot that flew the CIA's U-2 on its first operational photographic-intelligence mission, on 20 June 1956 (Mission 2003, see above). Multiple US sources claim that the USN's RF-8s collected better photographs than USAF's RF-101s.

5 Cold War encounters described in this sub-chapter combine the narratives provided by Isaev in *Pages of the History of the 32nd Guards Fighter Regiment*, with those of VFP-62, 'The Cuban Missile Crisis'. Characteristically, most of the Soviet pilots tended to identify almost every US tactical fighter that they sighted during the following engagement as a 'Voodoo', which though they sometimes were, most were not. In similar fashion, later on during the Vietnam War, Soviets deployed in North Vietnam tended to call every US fighter jet either a 'Thunderchief' (which would be the F-105), or more often a 'Phantom' (F-4), regardless of their actual type. Perhaps not to be outdone, US pilots generally considered any Soviet-made fighter jet a 'MiG'.

6 Dobbs, *One Minute to Midnight* & NSA, 'Interview with Grigory Romanovich Danilevich'.

7 Whitten et al, pp. 72-79.

8 Contrary to what is steadfastly reported in virtually all the US accounts of this incident, the damage to the two Crusaders was not limited to 'puffs of smoke visible in rear-view mirrors', and the related reports were forwarded all the way up to the White House. For details, see transcript of October 27 Cuban Missile Crisis ExComm Meetings, 10/27/62, p. 18; *U.S. Plane Cuba*, 10/27/62

9 Unless stated otherwise, this sub-chapter is based Dobbs, *One Minute to Midnight*.

10 The official nickname Delta Dagger was never used in common parlance: to its crews, the type was universally known as the 'Deuce'. While there is still some doubt whether the two F-102As involved in this incident were really armed with nuclear-tipped missiles, the fact that the USAF never released documentation related to this incident is strongly supportive for this version.

11 Newlin, 'The Case of the Runaway U-2'.

Chapter 8

1 Pedlow et al, *The Central Intelligence Agency and Overhead reconnaissance: the U-2 and OXCART Programs*.

2 Other changes included the decision to launch the development of a hypersonic reconnaissance aircraft – eventually resulting in the Lockheed SR-71 Blackbird – and to bolster the development and the use of reconnaissance satellites. However, both of these affairs are well outside the scope of this volume.

3 Unless stated otherwise, this chapter is based upon Pedlow & Welzenbach.

4 Gen. Hsichun Mike Hua http://roadrunnersinternationale.com/hua.html. Notably, at the time the town-council of Cortez was considering extinguishing the lights at the airport as a cost-saving measure. Fortunately for Hua, they were on that night.

5 Details of Taiwanese U-2 shootdowns described herein and in following sub-chapters are by large, though not exclusively, based on 'The Blackcat Squadron, U-2 Operation', *taiwanairpower.org* & 'The lost Black Cats', *zonaeuropa.com*

6 Unless stated otherwise, this chapter is based upon Gupta et al, 'The S-75 Dvina', and Tufail, *Against all Odds*.

7 Grimes, pp. 62-68.

8 Ultimately, the CIA developed a plan to deploy two battery-powered pods near Lop Nor. In the course of Operation Heavy Tea, a specially trained crew of the 34th Black Bat Squadron deployed these while flying a Lockheed C-130 Hercules transport of the USAF (with all national markings removed), on 17 May 1969. This time, the sensors worked and uploaded data on two of the PRC's nuclear tests, on 22 September 1969 and 29 September 1969, to a US intelligence satellite. For details, see Pocock, *The Black Bats*.

9 A tactical manual for this variant, issued by the Soviets to their export customers for the MiG-21F-13 in the early 1960s confidently – and extensively – discussed combat operations against supersonic aircraft (like the Convair B-58 Hustler) at altitudes up to 24,384m (80,000ft). For details, see *Fishbed C/E Aerial Tactics*, pp. 55-60, 69-70, 115, 120, 131-132.

10 *Aviatsiya i vremya* 2008/01

11 *Fishbed C/E Aerial Tactics*, p. 132.

12 Ibid, p. 132.

13 Gen. Hsichun Mike Hua, http://roadrunnersinternationale.com/hua.html. Yeh Chang-di and Chang Li-yi returned to Taiwan only in 1990.

14 Flintham, p. 77.

15 Roger Pessidous, 'Mirage vs U-2', aviateurs.e-monsite.com

Chapter 9

1 Delalande, 'Warning: MiG-25!'

2 ACIG.info forum

3 'Saudi Reconnaissance aircraft Shot down by Houthis', youtube.com; Cooper, *Hot Skies over Yemen*, pp. 44, 55-56, 61-63, 69.

4 This table is based on all available sources (see bibliography). The 'match-up' of serials for ROCAF U-2s was kindly provided by Chris Pocock: it is not based on any official records and thus remains 'uncertain', but was largely confirmed by Lai, *The Dragon's Teeth*, p. 33.

ABOUT THE AUTHOR

Krzysztof Dąbrowski from Poland has a lifelong interest in the subject of military aviation, and has written dozens of articles on a variety of related subjects for printed magazines and the ACIG.org/ACIG.info, AeroHisto and The Boresight websites. His particular area of interest is the air warfare during the Cold War, the aircraft involved, and the experiences of their crews. This is his first instalment for Helion.